CW01189612

*Green Hornets*

# Green Hornets

## The History of the U.S. Air Force 20th Special Operations Squadron

Wayne Mutza

Schiffer Military History
Atglen, PA

# Acknowledgments

When creating a book about people who made a notable impression upon American history, one of my goals is to have them pen their indelible recollections. Although some, understandably, are reluctant to resurrect memories of war, others took that trip back in time to relate what they did, and, often, how they felt about it. Most of the following men participated in the events that shaped the proud history of the Green Hornets, along with the Pony Express element. Without their help, this book would not have been possible.

My heartfelt thanks to Robert Arnau, Rodney Aukshun, James A. Ball, James Bedingfield, Tom Booth, Sean M. Borland, James W. Burns, Scott Buttrick, Waldon Byers, Charles A. Cantwell, Paul Cartter, Michael Collins, Carl Damonte, Darwin G. Edwards, Dale L. Eppinger, James Fudge, David J. Galvan, Tom Garcia, Leonard A. Gonzales, James W. Green, David Grossnickle, Kyron V. Hall, Geoff Hays, Jim Henthorn, Robert D. Hill, Raymond E. Hoffman, John Holt, Charles H. Isackson, Jr., Rich Jalloway, Paul Ray Jensen, Jerry Kibby, Thomas E. Kreidler, Chris Lenahan, Lennart Lundh, Virgil W. Magee, Hugh Mills, Robert W. Moore, James Pedriana, Richard J. Radeker, Dale K. Robinson, Phillip Rouviere, Nick Spain, David K. Sparks, Ron Thurlow, James R. Tolbert, Richard VanDerPloeg, James R. Wagner, Ronald C. Winkles, and Herbert R. Zehnder.

Book Design by Ian Robertson.

Copyright © 2007 by Wayne Mutza.
Library of Congress Control Number: 2007932937

All rights reserved. No part of this work may be reproduced or used in any forms or by any means – graphic, electronic or mechanical, including photocopying or information storage and retrieval systems – without written permission from the copyright holder.

Printed in China.
ISBN: 978-0-7643-2779-7

We are interested in hearing from authors with book ideas on related topics.

| Published by Schiffer Publishing Ltd. | In Europe, Schiffer books are distributed by: |
|---|---|
| 4880 Lower Valley Road | Bushwood Books |
| Atglen, PA 19310 | 6 Marksbury Avenue |
| Phone: (610) 593-1777 | Kew Gardens |
| FAX: (610) 593-2002 | Surrey TW9 4JF |
| E-mail: Info@schifferbooks.com. | England |
| Visit our web site at: www.schifferbooks.com | Phone: 44 (0) 20 8392-8585 |
| Please write for a free catalog. | FAX: 44 (0) 20 8392-9876 |
| This book may be purchased from the publisher. | E-mail: Info@bushwoodbooks.co.uk. |
| Please include $3.95 postage. | Free postage in the UK. Europe: air mail at cost. |
| Try your bookstore first. | Try your bookstore first. |

# Contents

Preface .................................................................................................................. 6
Introduction ......................................................................................................... 7

Chapter 1: Secret War ........................................................................................ 9
Chapter 2: Blue Suiters and Helicopters ............................................................ 12
Chapter 3: Into the Mouth of the Cat ................................................................. 16
Chapter 4: Above and Beyond ........................................................................... 52
Chapter 5: Between the Wars ............................................................................ 56
Chapter 6: Sandstorms ....................................................................................... 67

          Warriors ............................................................................................. 75
          Green Hornet Emblems ..................................................................... 114

Appendix A: Sikorsky CH-3C/E Helicopters Assigned to the 20th SOS ........... 127
Appendix B: Bell UH-1F/P Helicopters Assigned to the 20th SOS .................... 128
Appendix C: Bell UH-1N Helicopters Assigned to the 20th SOS ...................... 130
Appendix B: Sikorsky H-53 Helicopters Assigned to the 20th SOS ................... 132

          Bibliography ...................................................................................... 134

# Preface

The box finally arrived. It was well sealed, and the return label told me it was from "Jalloway's Glass" in Chicago. A couple years earlier, during my research for this book, Rich Jalloway and I played "phone tag," never solidly connecting. Eventually we corresponded, and with what he had placed in the box, Rich provided the explanation for the purpose of this book.

Atop a stack of about 100 photographs was a letter from Rich, along with a sheet of paper he had folded around a single photo. *This one must have special meaning*, I thought. Staring at me from the photo was a solidly built soldier, poised, confident, holding an M-16 rifle. The Asian wind blows his sandy colored hair, and presses his faded fatigues snug against his frame. Barely visible over the right breast pocket of his dirt-stained uniform is a name: "Fike." Above the pocket opposite is the lettering "U.S. Air Force," and above that, aircrew wings. In the background is the mount he rode to war—a camouflaged Huey helicopter of the 20th Special Operations Squadron, better known as the "Green Hornets." Jalloway wrote:

"As the years go by, the more I wonder about my old unit and all the men I was privileged to work with.

It's summer of 1970. I'm working on a flight line in Kansas for a Special Operations helicopter squadron. A new pilot walks up to one of our Hueys, and I greet him: 'Hi, I'm Airman Jalloway. Where you from?' He gives me the most distant stare I have ever seen. 'Captain Miller, just back from 20th SOS, Vietnam.' That's all he said as he boarded one of our Hueys and flew to one of our mission sites. I knew right then and there that I had to find out more. Three months later I'm a right door gunner in Vietnam in an outfit that's right out of Mars. I finally fit in somewhere in my life. Flying, protecting our crews, and the men we support, never really knowing who we work for, but who cares. It is one wild ride.

My memory is not the best as the years pass, but many things that happened there will always be with me. Even in my daily habits of going to work, raising a family, 'Nam is always with me. All the good and the bad.

Thomas E. Fike is part of my life. The last time we talked, December 4, 1971, he had only a couple of weeks left until discharge. He was my replacement flying out of Saigon. We talked for a while, and said our goodbyes. Later that day, when I was back at our camp, Fike's helicopter was shot down. He died that afternoon.

I have been to many vet get-togethers over the years, and I go for my friend Fike, to honor his sacrifice that day so long ago. I will always remember and honor all of our men. They are my brothers."

I couldn't have said it better. So, Rich, here's to you, and to Tom Fike, and to all your brothers—those who made it home, and those who didn't.

# Introduction

U.S. military personnel, including those of the U.S. Air Force, often were surprised to discover that the camouflaged helicopters with few identifying markings were Air Force aircraft flown by Air Force aircrew.

For a number of reasons, some military units pass into history with little fanfare, much less the credit due them for their accomplishments. Such has been the case with the 20th Special Operations Squadron—until now.

The 20th traces its lineage to 1942, when it was activated as the 20th Observation Squadron (Light) at Savannah Army Air Field, Georgia. Typical of many U.S. Air Force units, the 20th embarked on a vagabond-like journey that took it to various base assignments in North Carolina, Missouri, and Mississippi, while undergoing an equal number of designation changes. Finally, in December 1943, the 20th entered the war, flying missions in a variety of aircraft throughout India and Burma in support of the allied effort to reopen the Burma Road. At war's end, however, the squadron returned to the U.S. and was disbanded at Camp Kilmer, New Jersey. Its work with the 1st Air Commando Group during World War II foreshadowed the 20th's association with what has become popularly known as special operations.

As part of Air Force expansion into the field of rotary-wing aviation, the 20th Helicopter Squadron was activated on 9 July 1956, and attached to the 314th Troop Carrier Wing at Sewart Air Force Base, Tennessee. Equipped with Piasecki H-21 helicopters, the squadron flew airlift support missions throughout North America and Arctic regions. True to its reputation for operating units in a nomadic fashion, the Air Force in July 1959 relocated the 20th to Myrtle Beach AFB, South Carolina, where it was attached to the 354th Tactical Fighter Wing. The squadron was inactivated on 8 March 1960. A few years would pass before the unit would re-enter the pages of Air Force history.

It took the worsening situation in Southeast Asia for Air Force planners to realize, once again, that helicopters were needed to fulfill specific requirements. Sikorsky's CH-3 helicopter was relatively new to the Air Force, whose leaders viewed it as the ideal support aircraft for the expanding Search and Rescue (SAR) and counterinsurgency (COIN) missions, along with other tasks. In conjunction with a 1965 request by Air Force leaders in South Vietnam for more than two dozen CH-3C helicopters, the 20th was reactivated on 8 October. The following month a man named J.C. Horton took the unit, with ten CH-3Cs, to South Vietnam.

In February 1967 the CH-3Cs, which were nicknamed "Big Charlies," would be joined by the Air Force's own brand of the famed Bell "Huey" helicopter. Throughout the war the number of helicopters would increase, with improvements made in both types to keep pace with the ever-changing tactical environment. Unique to the "Pony Express" CH-3s and "Green Hornet" UH-1 Hueys were their roles in clandestine operations, evidenced in August 1968 by a designation change to the "20th Special Operations Squadron (SOS)."

## Green Hornets: The History of the U.S. Air Force 20th Special Operations Squadron

In a controversial move, the Air Force in 1969 transferred the CH-3s to the 21st SOS, while the Hueys continued to fly unconventional warfare missions. The switch to twin-engine UH-1N Hueys begun in 1970 was completed by the time the 20th was deactivated in March 1972.

Recognizing the importance of helicopters for special missions, and mindful of the lessons learned during the war in Southeast Asia, the Air Force in January 1976 reactivated the 20th SOS.

Undoubtedly, the U.S. government's interest in special operations during the post-war period prompted Air Force leadership to determine how it would play a key role. Its mix of CH-3s and Hueys once again helped the Air Force obtain a foothold in the world of shadow operations. As mission requirements and the structure of special operations changed by 1980, larger and more sophisticated Sikorsky H-53 helicopters replaced the CH-3s.

In 1983, Hueys of the 20th SOS began two years of involvement with drug enforcement, flying missions from the Bahamas. They were transferred in August 1985 to Homestead AFB, Florida, and in 1986 the unit received specially modified MH-53 "Pave Low" series helicopters.

Having proved the Pave Low's combat capability during *Operation Just Cause* in Panama during late 1989 and early 1990, the 20th in August 1990 became the first Air Force special operations forces to deploy during *Operation Desert Shield* in the Middle East.

While the activities of the 20th SOS in Afghanistan and Iraq at the time of this writing are necessarily kept under wraps, the modern Green Hornets continue the tradition of excellence in the spirit of those who went before them. Within these pages—in text, photographs, and in firsthand accounts—is the history of the Green Hornets. The complete story will never be told, not so much because certain secret documents may never be released, but because many of the participants no longer walk among us. This book emphasizes the details of the special *fling-wing* airmen who touched shoulders with the legendary men of SOG—whose own tales of courage did not become widely known until long after the war many would prefer to forget. But we should never forget.

# 1
# Secret War

More than three decades after the Vietnam war, no operations seem to stir more interest than those conducted secretly in Southeast Asia by the *Studies and Observation Group*, better known as *SOG*. The following overview of those activities in Southeast Asia will help to explain the role of U.S. Air Force helicopters in that no-longer-secret war.

The origins of SOG date back to the period following World War II, when America waded into the business of providing aid to Southeast Asian countries to prevent communist domination. In 1950 the United States began supplying economic and military aid to these governments, and by 1953 the growing U.S. military presence included nearly 300 advisors. Although this aid program was expanded after the 1954 Geneva Conference, advisors remained characterized as an extension of the U.S. diplomatic mission.

Due to the unstable political situation throughout Southeast Asia, the U.S. government firmly planted its feet in the region by creating the *Military Assistance Command Vietnam* (MACV) during February 1962. The U.S. Central Intelligence Agency (CIA) had been conducting and supporting clandestine operations throughout Southeast Asia for years with the blessing of President Eisenhower, who was bent on avoiding direct U.S. involvement. The CIA now had an official military command to support not only the steadily increasing number of advisors, but secret operations in North and South Vietnam, Laos, Cambodia, and southern China.

During the following decade, MACV and the CIA spawned and nurtured a vast, yet secret, network of units, whose size was determined by its specific mission. As this shadowy web grew, it teemed with code names and acronyms identifying objectives, locations, and units. The headquarters command itself, MACV, became so engrossed with clandestine operations that its title was lengthened to MACV-SOG in early 1964.

Central to clandestine operations in Southeast Asia was the U.S. Army Special Forces, also known as "Green Berets," or simply "SF." In 1964 it fell upon the SF to train and assist in the development of Vietnamese reconnaissance teams which, collectively, were known as *Project Delta*. The teams, which had been organized by the CIA, were to be slipped into Laos to conduct clandestine missions of surveillance, direct air strikes, and perform subsequent bomb damage assessment, rescue POWs, capture enemy soldiers, rescue downed airmen, place wire taps, plant booby-trapped ordnance, carry out assassinations, and generally harass the enemy on his own turf. These mission objectives would be adopted by succeeding recon teams. The teams, along with the helicopter crewmen, in whom they put their trust, called the missions "going across the fence."

The North Vietnamese clearly violated the Geneva Accords by running a major supply route to the south through Laos, prompting President Lyndon Johnson to authorize covert cross-border operations. Johnson, however, prohibited U.S. soldiers from participating in such missions. Without U.S. leadership and control, Project Delta's operation, dubbed *Leaping Lena*, failed after most of the Vietnamese commandos were killed or captured.

The lessons learned from Project Delta led to U.S.-led operations into Laos beginning in September 1965. Labeled *Operation Shining Brass*, these missions came under a new title, *Prairie Fire*, in 1968. Cambodia, in view of its avowed neutrality, was equally politically sensitive. However, since the North Vietnamese conducted operations within its borders, the U.S., beginning in 1967, sidestepped its observance of Cambodia's neutrality, and countered with secret missions into Cambodia, which were codenamed *Daniel Boone*, and later *Salem House*. Although Washington tacitly approved, the U.S. and South Vietnamese governments publicly denied cross-border operations.

SOG was a joint services arrangement comprising elements of all U.S. services, which were categorized under a Ground Studies Group, a Maritime Studies Group at Da Nang, an Air Studies Group at Nha Trang, a Psychological Studies Group at Saigon, and the MACV-SOG training center at Long Thanh. The Ground Studies Group launch sites were located at Hue-Phu Bai, Khe Sanh, Kham Duc, and near Kontum. Numerous other sites were used as staging areas, where teams were housed, and helicopters could be refueled and rearmed. Missions *across the fence* were also launched from U.S. air bases in Thailand.

MAVC-SOG eventually organized its ground elements into three field commands: Command and Control South, Central, and North (CCS, CCC, and CCN). Subordinate to these commands were teams of various sizes and functions. A platoon-size unit consisting of four or five SF men and about 40 indigenous soldiers was known as a *Hatchet Force*. The combination of two or more Hatchet Forces was called a *Havoc*, or *Hornet Force*. A *Mike Force* was 100 men strong. Another large SOG force was termed *SLAM*, for *Search, Locate, Annihilate, and Monitor*. *Bright Light* designated a rescue operation behind enemy lines.

Foremost among the mixture of units were more than 70 U.S. Army Special Forces Reconnaissance Teams (RTs) that were specially selected to carry out some of the most dangerous missions during the war. Recon teams of CCC were named for states, while those of CCN were named for poisonous snakes; teams of CCS were named for tools.

SOG teams comprised combinations of U.S.-led indigenous commandos, which were drawn from Laotian, Vietnamese, Cambodian, Montagnard, or Nung populations. Often they were mercenaries who were recruited and paid by SOG.

By 1967 nearly 300 recon missions had been launched into Laos, which prompted more than 80 missions using larger forces against targets uncovered by the teams. Being inserted by helicopters deep into enemy territory was extremely risky, and it took a special kind of soldier to survive and do it repeatedly. Since teams usually operated in supposedly neutral countries, U.S. identification was not carried nor worn, meaning that, if captured, they could expect to be treated as spies. Losses were high. It was a bad idea for Recon teams to make contact with the enemy or engage them in sustained combat.

Greatly outnumbered, instead they relied on stealth. SOG teams were one of the most effective weapons of the Vietnam conflict, not only because of their intelligence gathering capability, but also because they were a vexation to the North Vietnamese. Their engagement with the enemy, including air strikes they directed, resulted in a kill ratio estimated to be 150 to 1.

Recon teams, which initially were called *Spike Teams*, comprised between six and twelve men. Missions were scheduled to last seven to ten days, although they seldom lasted that long. The element of surprise quickly wore thin, and teams became the prey in deadly manhunts. The North Vietnamese were keenly aware that recon teams would attempt to probe deep within their territory. Experts at jungle warfare, the enemy had prepared an extensive network of Landing Zone (LZ) watchers, who monitored almost every area large enough to fit a helicopter into. The enemy also used specially trained trackers, some of whom used tracker dogs, to keep tabs on teams. And it was not unusual for the North Vietnamese to use communication equipment that intercepted team radio transmissions, thereby revealing their position.

A typical SOG recon team mission had the small group of commandos inserted by helicopter into an LZ, hopefully without being discovered. The mission goal and the area of operations dictated the number of helicopters and support aircraft used, which ranged from four to seven. Often, additional helicopters made false insertions distant from the original LZ with the hope of confusing the enemy. Another method of masking an insertion had the flight flying low over the LZ. The lead Huey dropped down to deposit the team, while the others flew overhead. When they passed, the insertion aircraft lifted to rejoin the procession at the rear, giving the impression that the flight had not altered its pattern. After hearing on the radio "Team Okay," the helicopters returned to the FOB, and the team made its way quietly to its objective. The chopper crew's wait to retrieve "their" team could last days, or end abruptly if the team was detected. In that event, the name of the game was to quickly break contact, evade, and dash to a pick-up zone (PZ) while calling for air support.

Typically, a U.S. Air Force Forward Air Controller (FAC) in a light aircraft was the team's only link to safety. The FAC crew comprised an experienced pilot and a seasoned SOG commando, called a *Covey Rider*; "Covey" was a common FAC call sign. FAC aircraft were either the O-1 "Bird Dog," O-2 "Skymaster," or OV-10 "Bronco." Orbiting a few miles away to prevent revealing the team's position, the FAC was the team's communications link; the FAC crew had the awesome responsibility of guiding the team, and handling air support if the team was on the run. If a helicopter LZ was unavailable, the next choice was snatching the team with rope ladders, or 120-foot long ropes, to which the commandos could attach a harness and be yanked up out of the jungle. Often, team members "rode the strings" as they were flown to safety back across the border.

If a team ran into trouble, the favored tactical air support aircraft was the A-1 "Skyraider." Able to withstand punishing anti-aircraft fire, and stay on station for hours, this piston-powered workhorse carried its own weight in ordnance, which often was placed "danger close" to the team by skilled Air Commando pilots. So reliable was their support that Skyraider squadrons specifically were assigned the SOG mission. Other air support assets included any armed aircraft, fixed-wing or helicopter, that was available, and able to respond to the FAC's call for assistance.

Helicopters tasked not only with inserting and extracting recon teams, but providing armed support, came from a variety of units. Flying almost exclusively for SOG was the Da Nang-based 219th Helicopter Squadron of the Vietnamese Air Force (VNAF). Fearless pilots of the 219th flew the aging Sikorsky H-34 helicopter, which came to be known in the SOG community as "Kingbee." When VNAF air assets were hard pressed to keep up with SOG's operational tempo, additional air support came from U.S. air units.

Flying in support of CCN recon teams were U.S. Marine Corps squadrons VMO-3 and HML-367. Owing to their sheer numbers of helicopters in Vietnam, and their familiarity with Special Forces, U.S. Army aviation units provided ample support of SOG missions. Most involved were nine units, all under the command of the 52nd Combat Aviation Battalion of the 1st Aviation Brigade, along with aviation elements of the 101st Airborne Division, beginning in 1968. These units typically flew SOG support for 60-day rotational periods.

In 1965 the 145th Airlift Platoon became the first Army helicopter unit assigned to Project Delta. It later merged with the 6th Aviation Platoon, flying UH-1 Huey gunships, to form the 2nd Platoon of the 171st Aviation Company. By July 1966 the 281st Assault Helicopter Company had assumed the 171st's assets, and trained as a special operations unit to be placed under operational control of the 5th Special Forces Group's Detachment B-52. Other Assault Helicopter Companies that provided SOG support were the 57th, 119th, 155th, 170th, 189th, 195th, and 282nd. In addition, the 361st Aviation Company (Escort), later called the 361st Aerial Weapons Company, was permanently assigned to support SOG units of CCC from 1968 through 1972.

Unique among the helicopter units that flew in support of SOG missions were the 20th and 21st Helicopter Squadrons of the U.S. Air Force. The 20th Special Operations Squadron "Green Hornets" would become the only USAF helicopter unit whose primary mission was the support of SOG recon teams. Like the skilled and courageous SOG men who placed their trust in them, the Green Hornets would make their mark in history.

# 2

# Blue Suiters and Helicopters

The union of the U.S. Air Force and helicopters occurred on 8 June 1944, when the Army Air Force accepted its first two Sikorsky R-4 helicopters. Their eventful flight, made from Sikorsky's Connecticut plant to Freeman Field, Seymour, Indiana, marked the beginning of a new era of aviation history. Although helicopter development was problematic, and the unique craft had yet to prove itself, Army Air Force leaders in late 1943 ordered 1,500 R-4s. With the order came the announcement that a helicopter training school was being established.

Initially formed at Freeman Field, and called the *Army Air Force Helicopter Training Detachment*, the school also earned the title *Gypsy School*, since it was moved nine times throughout its history.

Like a disfavored stepchild, the helicopter was viewed with skepticism by legions of aviators who were accustomed to aircraft with immovable wings. Although the future of the fling-wing variety of aircraft remained uncertain when the U.S. Air Force came into its own in 1947, they were flying machines nonetheless, and surely could prove of some use. It took the Korean war to prove the value of helicopters in the Air Force, particularly for rescue and clandestine operations.

The school's nomadic movements did not affect its growth or effectiveness, and the R-4 was phased out as Sikorsky's more powerful H-5 and R-6 became available.

Eventually the Bell H-13, Hiller H-23, Sikorsky H-19 and H-34, and Piasecki's H-21 were added. Only the H-19 and H-21 comprised frontline units.

Long before the famed Huey helicopter joined the Air Force, Sikorsky's H-19, developed in 1949, pioneered clandestine helicopter operations during the Korean war. The H-19 equipped the short-lived Helicopter Transport Force, and was put to greater use for missile site support and rescue. This H-19B was assigned to the Rescue Section at Albrook AFB, Canal Zone, during the 1950s. (U.S. Air Force)

## Chapter 2: Blue Suiters and Helicopters

The 20th Helicopter Squadron was formed in 1956 with Piasecki H-21 helicopters, which performed frontline service in North America and Arctic regions until the unit was inactivated in 1960. The H-21 was appropriately named the "Workhorse." (Boeing Vertol)

Optimistic about the helicopter's potential, Air Force leaders during the early 1950s formed a transport helicopter force. Unfortunately, the Air Force had a critical shortage of helicopter pilots, since the school also trained Army helicopter pilots, who far outnumbered Air Force graduates due to an expanding Army helicopter inventory. The pilot shortage, combined with the Army's establishment of its own training program—plus its procurement of large numbers of troop-carrying helicopters—spelled the end of the Air Force helicopter transport force. The business of helicopter airlift, Air Force leaders felt, was best left to the Army and Marine Corps. Besides, Air Force planners were more interested in developing Cold War airpower requirements, and re-directed their focus on helicopters best suited for utility work and search and rescue.

To fulfill those needs, the Air Force chose Kaman's H-43A, which proved ideal for the *Local Base Rescue* mission. The piston-powered H-43A, the first of which arrived in 1958, gave way to the

After the U.S. Navy pioneered the use of Sikorsky's twin-turbine S-61, the Air Force in 1962 borrowed three SH-3As from the Navy and purchased three S-61As, all of which were designated CH-3Bs. This S-61A was one of three supporting the Texas Tower radar sites from Otis AFB, Massachusetts. (Joe Ballinger Collection)

turbine-powered H-43B. Sikorsky's twin-turbine CH-3B, which had its equivalent in the Navy SH-3A, appeared in 1962. It was replaced by the rear-ramp CH-3C, the first of which was delivered to the Tactical Air Command in 1964. The CH-3C provided the Air Force not only with an all-weather, longer range, and more powerful helicopter, but one that offered a large payload capability.

The arrival of Bell's revolutionary UH-1 *Huey* design was the final step in converting to an all-turbine-powered helicopter fleet. The first two UH-1F models were turned over to the 4486th Test Squadron at Eglin AFB, Florida, in September 1964. Based on Bell's short-fuselage Model 204, the UH-1F featured an unusual engine arrangement to absorb an abundance of GE T-58 engines used to power Air Force CH-3s. To accommodate the engine the exhaust was routed to the right side, and a gearbox reduced RPM and changed the direction of drive 180 degrees. The unique engine configuration used the larger main rotor of the long-fuselage Model 205, which, in turn, required use of the 205's stretched tail boom. At its mission gross weight of 9,000 pounds, the F Model had a maximum speed of 120 mph and a range of 347 miles. It could carry one pilot and ten passengers, or two pilots and 2,000

The CH-3C, which introduced a stretched fuselage and rear cargo ramp, first went to the Tactical Air Command in 1963. The type soon found a home in air rescue and special operations. (National Archives)

## Chapter 2: Blue Suiters and Helicopters

The first of 120 UH-1Fs produced by Bell Helicopter for the U.S. Air Force. All UH-1Fs were delivered in overall dark blue with white cabin roofs. (Bell Helicopter)

pounds of cargo. A total of 119 UH-1Fs were delivered, along with 27 TH-1F trainer variants, which joined the school's HH-43B and CH-3C in 1967.

As intended, the Huey mainly supported missile bases, while the CH-3C carried out heavy utility work assignments. The increase in America's involvement in the war in Southeast Asia saw the HH-43B premier in the firefighting and rescue role, while the Huey and the CH-3C found a home in the shadowy world of special operations. The rescue version of the CH-3, the HH-3E, would prove itself a star performer in Air Rescue as the *Jolly Green Giant*, along with its replacement, the larger and more powerful HH-53.

As the war placed increasing demands on the Air Force to produce helicopter pilots, beginning in 1971 USAF helicopter pilots received their preliminary training under Army sponsorship at Fort Rucker, Alabama. Advanced training was conducted at the 1550th Aircrew Training and Test Wing (ATTW) at Hill AFB, Utah. In 2004 the Air Force again assumed responsibility for the complete training of its helicopter pilots.

Long before Air Force Hueys were considered for the gunship role, the Tactical Air Command experimentally modified this early UH-1F with an M-60 machine gun system then common on Army Hueys. (Bell Helicopter)

# 3

## Into the Mouth of the Cat

**Thailand**

The introduction of the 20th Special Operations Squadron to the war in Southeast Asia, like many Air Force pursuits, was multifaceted. Throughout the war, elements of the squadron, comprising CH-3 and UH-1 helicopters, underwent changes to keep pace with tactical requirements.

The 20th Helicopter Squadron was established at Ton San Nhut Air Base, South Vietnam, on 8 October 1965. It was first equipped with CH-3Cs, some of which were inherited from the 4401st Helicopter Squadron of the Tactical Air Command at Eglin AFB. The 4401st had been temporarily deployed in July 1965 to Nakhon Phanom (NKP) Royal Thai Air Force Base (RTAFB), Thailand, to augment search and rescue assets. By year's end the 20th HS boasted 14 CH-3Cs, which were organized into detachments to meet mission requirements. Detachment A at Tan Son Nhut had five aircraft, Detachment B at Da Nang used three, and Detachment C at Nha Trang operated six. Herb Zehnder, who was assigned to Da Nang, recalls:

"We worked with the Marines and the Army most of the time. During the time I worked with the Marines we mainly hauled 105 howitzers, and food stuffs going to pick up the howitzers."

In February 1966 two CH-3Cs and crews were moved to NKP, where they formed D Flight, which became known as the *Pony Express*, conducting covert missions in Laos and Thailand. Zehnder continues:

"Based at NKP, we did most of our work out of bases to the east, that is, infiltration and exfiltration. Most of the missions were flown at night, without the proper navigation facilities. How and why I managed to put the people in the right spot is beyond belief. Picking people up was a snap, because they knew we were coming, and there was little doubt as to who they were, as they were anxious to get out."

Members of the 606th ACS, from which the 20th Helicopter Squadron evolved, pose in Thailand. The UH-1F behind them is in stateside condition, complete with blue paint and the familiar white cabin roof. Left to right are: crew chief SGT William Slack, Operations Officer Capt. William Clark, the governor of Chaing Rai, pilot Lt. Richard Madigan, Instructor Pilot Capt. Tom Garcia, and crew chief SGT Brown. (Tom Garcia Collection)

## Chapter 3: Into the Mouth of the Cat

Wearing body armor, a Green Hornet gunner mans the rudimentary door gun arrangement of a UH-1F in 1966. Suspended with straps top and bottom, the infantry style M-60A machine gun has a long rod attached to the barrel to prevent firing into the aircraft. Special Forces SOG Recon Team leader MSGT Gilreath sits in the cabin doorway. Visible on the Huey's doorpost is the name "Ginny." (Tom Garcia)

When the 20th was assigned to the newly activated 14th Air Commando Wing (ACW) at Nha Trang in March, it was averaging nearly 1,000 sorties per month.

During the first quarter of 1966, the 20th HS dedicated eight CH-3Cs to supporting U.S. Marines during *Operation Double Eagle*, the largest amphibious assault since the Korean war. During a major battle for the Special Forces camp in the A Shau Valley on 9 March, a 20th CH-3C crew withstood heavy fire to land inside the camp, rescuing a downed Marine helicopter crew and 35 wounded. It was during this battle that Major Bernie Fisher earned the Medal of Honor by landing his A-1 Skyraider to rescue a downed flyer.

In April the Nha Trang detachment was moved to Udorn RTAFB in northern Thailand, followed by the Da Nang detachment in May. These moves satisfied the Thai government's desire to bolster the counterinsurgency efforts of its military and police forces. With the majority of its assets in Thailand, the 20th HS became engrossed in the serious business of cross-border missions, often in support of Laotian General Vang Pao's guerillas. Using the call sign "Pony," Pony Express crews quickly became adept at inserting, supplying, and extracting SOG teams in Laos. During the first five months of operations in Thailand, the 20th flew nearly 400 commandos into or out of Laos. Missions flown by the 20th were under direct control of the CIA, and usually included protective escort by Thailand-based Skyraiders.

Although launching from Thailand allowed the 20th to penetrate farther north into enemy strongholds, the first infiltration mission into North Vietnam was launched from South Vietnam in June 1966. By year's end the Pony Express had carried out 315 infiltration sorties. The unit's unconventional warfare role would gain even more momentum with the introduction of a completely different type of helicopter, along with a few pilots who were skilled at flying them.

### Enter the Huey

While the Pony Express crews and their CH-3C Big Charlies were making history throughout Southeast Asia, another aspect of the unit was taking shape. The American response to the deteriorating situation in Vietnam included plans by Air Force leaders for a

MSGT McClendon, the Green Hornet maintenance NCO at Ban Me Thuot, demonstrates the Slick gunners' position during team infiltrations and extractions. Getting out on the skids allowed for rapid troop loading/offloading, and gave the gunner more latitude during the crucial time in the landing zone. The early Sagami gun mount incorporating the infantry model M-60A machine gun was unique to Army Hueys. (U.S. Air Force)

# Green Hornets: The History of the U.S. Air Force 20th Special Operations Squadron

Although psychological operations (psy-ops) was a cover story used to explain the 20th's existence, no record exists of Green Hornet Hueys mounting speaker systems, such as that being tested on this early model UH-1F. (Bell Helicopter)

counterinsurgency force to support Special Forces. Unfortunately, such plans were not part of the blueprint for a modern all-jet Air Force. Nevertheless, President Kennedy, acting on statements made by Russian and North Vietnamese leaders, directed that the military develop ways of dealing with unconventional warfare. The Air Force complied by forming the 4400th Combat Crew Training Squadron, nicknamed "Jungle Jim." It was replaced in April 1962 by the Special Air Warfare Center, which was responsible for training *Air Commandos*. The center spawned the 606th Air Commando Squadron (ACS), comprising five types of single-engine and twin-engine prop-driven aircraft: L-20 Beaver, U-10 Helio Courier, T-28 Trojan, C-123 Provider, and A-26 Invader. It was intended that the 606th ACS supplement Thai air assets, and train Thai forces in counterinsurgency.

The usefulness of helicopters in counterinsurgency, especially in regions with severe weather and impassable terrain, had been recognized two decades earlier. The Royal Thai government believed that their greatest handicap in combating an increase in insurgency in 1966 was an insufficient number of helicopters. Preferring not to increase American troop strength in Thailand, Ambassador to Thailand Graham Martin instead committed a few more USAF helicopters to expedite Royal Thai Air Force helicopter training. Therefore, in addition to the CH-3Cs sent to Thailand, four UH-1F helicopters, which were culled from Strategic Air Command (SAC) missile site support units, were added to the inventory of the 606th ACS.

In anticipation of expanded enemy infiltration through Laos, U.S. officials began fielding more roadwatch teams, which com-

Pilot Raymond Hoffman was seriously injured when this UH-1F crashed during a Montagnard training mission at White Castle Special Forces Camp in 1967. Pilot Robert Berka was also injured, and a Montagnard soldier was killed. (Tom Garcia)

## Chapter 3: Into the Mouth of the Cat

CH-3Cs of the 20th's *Pony Express* undergo maintenance at Udorn RTAFB in 1968. The aircraft at right has its national insignia placard inserted upside down in a rack designed for easy insignia removal. (Kyron Hall)

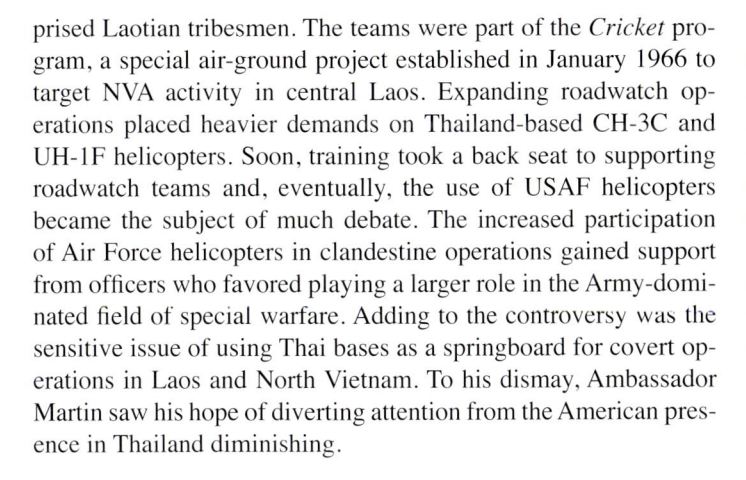

Green Hornet aircrew enjoy cigars prior to rotating out of Ban Me Thuot East. Transportation in and out of "BMT" was provided by C-123 and C-130 *Blackbirds*. At lower left is Capt. Bruce Knapp, next to Capt. James Wagner. (James R. Wagner Collection)

prised Laotian tribesmen. The teams were part of the *Cricket* program, a special air-ground project established in January 1966 to target NVA activity in central Laos. Expanding roadwatch operations placed heavier demands on Thailand-based CH-3C and UH-1F helicopters. Soon, training took a back seat to supporting roadwatch teams and, eventually, the use of USAF helicopters became the subject of much debate. The increased participation of Air Force helicopters in clandestine operations gained support from officers who favored playing a larger role in the Army-dominated field of special warfare. Adding to the controversy was the sensitive issue of using Thai bases as a springboard for covert operations in Laos and North Vietnam. To his dismay, Ambassador Martin saw his hope of diverting attention from the American presence in Thailand diminishing.

Under code name *Project Lucky Tiger*, the 606th ACS was deployed to NKP, followed shortly thereafter in August 1966 by six air-delivered UH-1Fs. Six pilots and a group of mechanics arrived a few days later. Less than one week later they were joined by 29 temporary duty pilots and more maintenance personnel. Although they were part of the 606th ACS, they were also considered a detachment of the 20th HS, and often referred to as *E Flight*.

The UH-1Fs arrived in Thailand wearing the SAC scheme of dark blue with a white cabin roof. Eventually they were repainted in camouflage schemes at NKP. To downplay the American presence in Thailand, and in the futile hope of ensuring deniability, all markings were left off of the aircraft except for a partial serial number on the tail fin and nose in black, and later, a black or green hornet stenciled on the tail boom.

A Pony Express CH-3 flies low over the Mekong River northwest of Udorn in April 1968. (Kyron Hall)

## Green Hornets: The History of the U.S. Air Force 20th Special Operations Squadron

Although the UH-1Fs and crews were assigned to the Thai government, their mission orders came from the 7th/13th Air Force Mission Coordination Center in Bangkok. Services provided by the Thai government included the military, Border Police, Department of Highways, and the health department. The duties of these agencies overlapped, meaning that UH-1F crews simply chose whatever insignia to attach to their Huey's tail boom. So much of the war was fought in the shadows that eventually countless aircraft were fit with holders for removable insignia. Some cargo swapping and a few extra marks on the map enabled the UH-1F crews to swap missions with *Air America*.

As the CIA's secretly owned airline, Air America was a vital component in the Agency's ambitions in Laos. Although the CIA was largely responsible for military operations in Laos, Ambassador to Laos William Sullivan was in charge. Sullivan closely monitored military operations in Laos, insisting that no regular U.S. ground troops be involved, and that operations be conducted in secrecy, to support the illusion of compliance with the Geneva Accords. Eventually Air America owned about 50 fixed-wing aircraft and 30 helicopters, the latter consisting mainly of Sikorsky H-34s and Bell Hueys. The wide range of missions flown by Air America crews—who wore civilian clothing, and flew relatively unmarked aircraft—included medevac, rescuing downed aircrew, supporting roadwatch teams, monitoring sensors along infiltration routes, transporting troops and refugees, and conducting photo reconnaissance.

Tom Garcia was one of the original six UH-1F pilots, having been transferred from SAC's 341st Combat Support Group at Malstrom AFB, Montana, where he flew missile site support. He recalls how the Air Force helicopter crews, like those of Air America, flew "sterile" missions; that is, void of anything that identified them as Americans if they were killed or captured. Prior to going on missions in Laos, U.S. military personnel turned in their dog tags and military identification cards. Garcia adds:

A 20th Helicopter Squadron CH-3C delivers a generator to a camp in northern Laos in 1967. Like all Pony Express CH-3s, s/n 64-14222 carried its partial serial number on the lower nose to aid ground troops in loading. (Alton Deviney)

The XM-93 minigun system left little room in the UH-1P's cabin for anything other than two gunners. The universal mount to which the rocket launcher was attached was the same as that used on U.S. Army gunships. (Jim Burns)

Thirty-foot rope ladders dangle from a UH-1F Slick preparing to pick up a recon team. (James Pedriana)

## Chapter 3: Into the Mouth of the Cat

A Green Hornet UH-1P is framed in the windshield of a sister ship flying tight formation in 1970. (James Pedriana)

"I remember those missions, and have photos I took in Laos. There we were in civilian clothes, and with an unmarked made-in-the-USA helicopter in the background. It was really a sham. At one point I mulled over the idea of telling any bad guys who showed up that we were Canadians with the International Control Commission.

There was one thing I forgot to turn in. The briefers never thought to ask, 'You guys got any tattoos?' Maybe my Indian motorcycle logo would not have been easily recognized by an Asian, but the Indian chief tattoo might have blown my cover. Well, there are Indians in Canada. The tattoo on my other arm would have done me in for sure: a prop and wings, a U.S. flag, and the lettering 'USAF.'"

There was no shortage of work for the UH-1Fs. Although the crews were of non-combatant status, pilot Ray Hoffman states, "Supporting a Thai operation against insurgents, we picked up ground fire and received battle damage." Garcia adds, "When we received decorations, which were usually for action in Laos or Cambodia, the citation always said 'Republic of Vietnam.'" Periodically the USAF crews participated in large scale COIN efforts by the Thai government. On 8 August 1966, for example, eight UH-1Fs and a CH-3C airlifted 350 Thai troops moving against an insurgent stronghold. Search and rescue missions to recover downed aircrew in Laos were common. Huey crews also were kept busy flying in support of visiting U.S. and Thai military and political officials, including President Johnson.

A Slick gunner straps on body armor in preparation for a mission from Ban Don in July 1970. This gunner wears his .38 cal. revolver where crewmen often desired extra protection. (James Pedriana)

# Green Hornets: The History of the U.S. Air Force 20th Special Operations Squadron

Caught in the act. 20th SOS crewmen apply their Green Hornet "zap" to an Army AH-1G Cobra of the 334th Aerial Weapons Company. (Rich Jalloway)

SGT Rivero-Torres displays the infantry type M-79 40mm grenade launcher commonly carried by aircrew as a backup weapon. In plain view is the later style Sagami mount for the M-60A. (Rich Jalloway)

Civic action duties played a large part in flying activities. Two UH-1Fs assigned to work the massive flood of the Mekong River were often overloaded to evacuate civilians.

On one of those flights, Ray Hoffman set a world record with his nine-passenger UH-1F by carrying 34 flood victims, plus a crew of three. The fact that the feat was accomplished with a normal takeoff spoke highly of the F Model's power.

U.S. officials, relying on evidence indicating that enemy aircraft were flying over Thailand, increased night intercept capabilities, using 606th helicopters as training targets. Huey pilots in Thailand heard reports of communist helicopters re-supplying troops in northern Thailand at night. One exuberant pilot wanted to intercept them and then fly alongside and shoot them down, or fly above them and drop chains into their rotors.

Since the State and Defense departments determined that Thai counterinsurgency training could be completed by the end of 1966, they ordered that all USAF helicopters be withdrawn from Thailand by the end of January 1967. Some felt the Thais could go it alone, however, the Air Force position against pulling them out was backed by Ambassador Sullivan. After warning Defense Secretary McNamara that conditions in Laos would deteriorate if the helicopters were withdrawn, Sullivan won his appeal. The Joint Chiefs of Staff then directed that ten CH-3Cs remain in Thailand, along with four UH-1Fs, solely for missions into Laos and North Vietnam. The remaining 21 aircraft, 15 of which were UH-1Fs, were sent to Vietnam. Prior to departure, the unit christened itself the "Green Hornets." Temporary duty personnel returned to their stateside units, and the six original pilots, along with enlisted

20th SOS crewmen look over the grim crash site of UH-1F s/n 63-13155, which was lost on 21 October 1969. (Alfonse Rivero-Torres)

As the crewman aboard a covering chopper, Jim Burns photographed this UH-1F on fire and going down in 1967. Its speed decreaser gear box had exploded, causing the fire. The gear box was the powerful engine's Achilles' heel, especially when it overheated. The crew of four and six-man SOG team escaped injury.

## Chapter 3: Into the Mouth of the Cat

Green Hornet helicopters shared the unfriendly skies of Laos with Air America helicopters, often flying the same missions as the CIA-owned aircraft. This Bell 204 flies near unmarked CH-34s at a remote fueling site, called an FOL. (James R. Wagner)

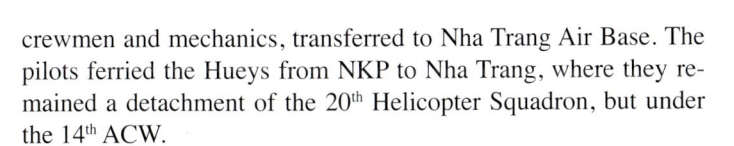

Combat damage and the abrasive laterite dust of Southeast Asia took their toll on helicopter rotor blades, and often replacement blades could be brought to remote areas only by chopper. Transporting rotor blades in this manner required great flying skill. (Craig Szwed)

crewmen and mechanics, transferred to Nha Trang Air Base. The pilots ferried the Hueys from NKP to Nha Trang, where they remained a detachment of the 20th Helicopter Squadron, but under the 14th ACW.

### Vietnam

Shortly after returning to their U.S. bases, most of the temporary duty personnel received orders sending them back to Southeast Asia, this time to Nha Trang. Tom Garcia had volunteered to stay with the Huey section for the transfer to Nha Trang, but was denied:

"Upon my arrival back at Malstrom," Garcia says, "Guess what I found? Orders to Nha Trang as a Huey pilot. And, what I had been most anxious to avoid: Winter Survival School at Fairchild AFB, Washington—just what I needed for Southeast Asia. I had already done the winter course in Labrador, plus the Swamp Rat School in Florida, complete with POW camp. After Fairchild it was another survival camp in the Philippines. Finally, on to Saigon."

After the move to Nha Trang, several UH-1Fs were shipped from the U.S. to Vietnam, boosting the Green Hornet inventory to more than 20 Hueys. Those not already camouflaged were painted

Prior to a mission Slick gunners don "monkey harnesses," which kept them from falling free of the aircraft. The UH-1F's stretched tail boom allowed for a baggage compartment. Unfortunately, its location directly below the exhaust often made it difficult to access. The UH-1F's original bell-mouth engine air inlet drew so much dirt into the engine that it was replaced by the particle separator system seen here behind the rotor head. (James Pedriana)

## Green Hornets: The History of the U.S. Air Force 20th Special Operations Squadron

A gunner loads 2.75-inch high explosive warhead rockets into a seven-tube launcher. Resting atop the launcher mount is an armored torso protector, referred to as a "chicken plate." (David Galvan)

A Green Hornet flight headed for trouble in July 1970. Flights inbound to the mission area were usually flown above 4,000 feet, but the Hueys worked at treetop level during team infiltrations and extractions. (James Pedriana)

in-country. Initially the Hueys were armed with two infantry-type M-60 machine guns suspended in the cabin doorways with bungee cords. This arrangement allowed the gunners so much latitude that a long metal rod was attached to the weapon's barrel to prevent an overzealous gunner from shooting the aircraft.

Eventually the UH-1Fs were locally modified with Sagami mounts, which were first fabricated for Army Hueys, and featured the M-60 swivel-mounted atop a swing-out mount.

As the only combat UH-1 helicopter squadron in the Air Force, the Vietnam-based Green Hornets went to work for the 5th Special Forces. SOG chief Colonel Jack Singlaub endorsed the arrangement, citing the experience of Green Hornet pilots. Unlike the typical 21-year-old Army Huey pilot, many 20th pilots were much older officers, and highly experienced. Nor was it lost on the SOG community that Air Force Hueys had a more powerful engine, meaning greater payloads and faster escapes from enemy lairs.

SGT Sully, the non-commissioned officer in charge of gunners during 1970, demonstrates the gunner's position during combat. This precarious stance outside the aircraft leaves little doubt as to the need for the monkey harness. (David Galvan)

Painted in broad bands of the Air Force Southeast Asia color scheme, UH-1P s/n 65-7930 flies over jungle in 1970. (James Pedriana)

## Chapter 3: Into the Mouth of the Cat

With "Kingbee" CH-34s nearby, 20th SOS aircrew pass the time at Thieu Atar in 1971 after having inserted a SOG team. It was vital that the same aircrew that inserted a team be the same crew to pull it out. (James R. Wagner)

20th SOS aircrew look on as Special Forces soldiers interrogate a prisoner at Duc Co in 1968. (Jim Tolbert)

SOG teams supported by the Green Hornets were comprised mainly of indigenous soldiers. To give them an edge in enemy territory, team members, such as this native armed with an AK-47, resembled the enemy. (Rich Jalloway)

Enhancing the SOG-Green Hornet partnership was the fact that 20th crewmen lived with SOG teams, which fostered a strong working relationship and rapport. Green Hornet crews rotated every ten days to the CCS camp at Ban Me Thuot, their mode of transportation usually being special operations C-123 or C-130 "Blackbirds." Since, logistically, the squadron had to be close to its main support base (Nha Trang), seldom did it draw large assignments beyond the central highlands, where Ban Me Thuot, or "BMT," was located. Marine units flew SOG missions in the northern regions, and the Army flew the missions for SOG teams to the south.

Before additional pilots were channeled into the squadron, the original six shouldered the load, supplemented by CH-3C pilots from the 20th's Udorn detachment. Prior to using CH-3C pilots as Huey copilots, the Air Force had allowed crew chiefs to serve in that capacity. Using non-Huey qualified CH-3C pilots drew harsh criticism after the 20th suffered its first casualty on 31 March 1967.

On that day about 130 troops, including their American advisors, were surrounded in Laos by an estimated 700 enemy soldiers. Casualties had been heavy, and they were nearly out of water and ammunition. The guns were quickly removed from four Green Hornet UH-1Fs, three of which had hoists installed. Aboard the lead Huey was Major Robert Baldwin, who was the flight commander, CH-3 pilot David Lyall as copilot, crew chief Russell Hunt, gunner Sandy Pratcher, and an SF medic.

Army helicopter gunships had drawn heavy fire, and a FAC had called in Skyraiders to silence heavy weapons. When Baldwin asked his crew if they wanted to go in, they responded with, "Okay, let's go for broke." As Baldwin eased the Huey into a 100-foot hover over a hole in the jungle canopy, and Hunt began to lower the hoist saddled with canteens and ammo boxes, all hell broke loose! Baldwin took a 12.7mm round in the gut and the chopper crashed, almost on top of the wounded Army team leader, who was to ride the hoist out.

# Green Hornets: The History of the U.S. Air Force 20th Special Operations Squadron

UH-1P crew chief Jim Pedriana rains fire on the enemy in February 1970. (James Pedriana Collection)

CH-3 s/n 63-9676 of the 20th's Pony Express element in Thailand undergoes maintenance in 1965. Wearing an overall dark blue scheme with high visibility markings and artwork on the cabin door, she later gained notoriety when painted all black and named "Black Mariah." Jack Meacham, who flew CH-3s with the 20th HS, says that Mariah was painted black only because they were out of regular paint, and thereafter the crews didn't want it changed. (U.S. Air Force)

As Skyraiders laid down ordnance, buying time for those on the ground, Captain Robert Allen moved his UH-1F in for a rescue attempt. Heavy gunfire drove him off, making it obvious the ground party would have to move away from the guns. While engaged in a firefight with the closing enemy, Lyall and Pratcher were wounded. With Skyraiders placing ordnance *danger close*, Hunt and Pratcher carried Baldwin, who was now unconscious, toward a bomb crater where choppers could get in. Baldwin succumbed to his wounds before the first Huey lined up for the tight approach. Robert Allen describes what he saw:

"When I brought my chopper back in, there stood Hunt, cool as a crew chief on a stateside ramp, waving me down through the trees and bamboo surrounding the clearing he had helped make. As soon as I loaded he waved me off, and I left him with the small arms fire popping around the perimeter not much more than a hundred feet away. Still standing, Hunt guided in the second and third Hueys the same way. Not until he got the most seriously wounded aboard did he come out on the third aircraft."

For his actions, Sergeant Hunt became the second living enlisted airman to earn the Air Force Cross, which is surpassed only by the Medal of Honor. Major Baldwin also received the award. Affirming the high risk nature of Green Hornet missions, just one month earlier, Captain John Gruver had flown a mission during which he made multiple gun passes to cover a search and rescue effort and rescue wounded, earning him the Air Force Cross.

CH-3E s/n 63-9678 after it crashed at the mountaintop Lima Site (LS)-85 in Laos on 30 December 1967. (Kyron Hall)

## Chapter 3: Into the Mouth of the Cat

Black Mariah and an unmarked CH-53 refuel at LS-36 in Laos in March 1968. (Kyron Hall)

After Baldwin's death, support of Special Forces lost momentum; however, the crews were kept busy training and working with the Navy's *Operation Market Time*, which was intended to stem enemy infiltration by sea. In the meantime, UH-1Fs modified as gunships were arriving from the States, replacing earlier models, which were shipped back for modification. Gunship versions received hard points that accommodated a pair of GAU-2B/A crew-operated miniguns, and two LAU-59/A 2.75-inch, seven-tube rocket launchers. The rocket launcher mounts initially were of the XM-156 type, familiar to Army Huey gunships, which incorporated the M-60 Sagami apparatus. They were eventually replaced by a more compact mount of the type seen on U.S. Marine Corps Hueys. The 7.62mm miniguns comprised the XM-93 system, and featured a rate of fire of either 2,000 or 4,000 rounds per minute. The guns could be locked for forward firing by the pilot.

The aircraft received special radios, along with a KY-28 speech security system, known as "Seek Silent," which prevented enemy eavesdropping. The device was located in the Huey's bat-

A 20th SOS CH-3 at the "Channel 99" radar site at Savannaket, Laos, in March 1968. Pony Express crews made every effort to avoid having to stay at such sites overnight. (Kyron Hall)

Although Black Mariah was said to be the only black-painted CH-3 of the war, it's likely that this photo shows another darkly painted CH-3 which, reportedly, was lost shortly after it arrived in the war zone. The mystery CH-3, which sports the removable national insignia, is seen here at NKP in the fall of 1965. (U.S. Air Force)

## Green Hornets: The History of the U.S. Air Force 20th Special Operations Squadron

A Green Hornet UH-1P at the Duc Lap border outpost. Its location near the Cambodian border made Duc Lap an ideal launch site for cross-border operations. (Darwin Edwards)

tery compartment, and had to be removed in the event an aircraft was downed to prevent its falling into enemy hands. Other modifications, which included armor pilot seats and self-sealing fuel tanks, were extensive enough to warrant the new designation UH-1P. Most Green Hornet UH-1Fs were brought up to UH-1P standards and, eventually, unit records listed all the aircraft as UH-1Ps. Those lacking heavy armament systems, but still sporting M-60s, were called "Slicks," a term borrowed from the Army to identify troop transport Hueys.

By May 1967 additional pilots had arrived, and the support of Special Forces again became the unit's primary mission. The five original pilots left in August 1967, and Thailand-based temporary duty pilots continued to fill *left-seat* shortages throughout the year.

With an increasing workload came more casualties. In late 1967 a UH-1F crashed during a Montagnard training mission at White Castle SF Base near Kontum. One Montagnard was killed, and the pilots, Raymond Hoffman and Robert Berka, were seriously injured. Another 1967 crash during a training mission, this one west of Nha Trang, injured Green Hornet pilots Lacy, Piesher, and Yontek. Gunship pilot Royal Foster describes what happened to him during the December 1967 battle of Ban Me Thuot:

"I was coming off the target. Everything was fine, except the ship wasn't flying right. The nose was way off to the right, and I couldn't get any airspeed. My copilot punched the interphone and said, 'Why are you holding so much right rudder?' And I saw that

Nothing was exempt from the Green Hornet zap, including crew chief David Galvan's cast after he was injured in a crash. (David Galvan Collection)

The rocket launchers of this UH-1P, seen at Ban Don in June 1970, bore the name "Whirly Bird 7." (James Pedriana)

## Chapter 3: Into the Mouth of the Cat

*During 1968 nearly all 20th SOS Hueys wore nose art. This was the artwork of crew chief SGT Fisher. (James Tolbert)*

*To SOG teams, a Green Hornet Slick landing on their smoke was a welcome view. (James Pedriana)*

I had full right rudder." (Although the common term was "right pedal," Air Force helicopter pilots were fixed-wing pilots first, and continued to use fixed-wing terms).

Foster then realized he had been shot in the leg, was in a lot of pain, and was involuntarily keeping his right leg stiff against the tail rotor pedal. With great difficulty he removed his leg from the pedal, the crew chief applied a tourniquet, and his copilot flew him to the Nha Trang hospital.

The 20th's CH-3 element in Thailand, meanwhile, also remained in the thick of things. Later in the year a handful of CH-3s had been returned to Thailand from Vietnam for *Project Igloo White*, dropping sensors along the infamous Ho Chi Minh Trail. One of the Big Charlie pilots, Major Kyron Hall, in November 1967 became the first man in the Air Force to complete 6,000 hours of flying time in helicopters. The following are some of Hall's recollections of his time with the 20th:

"Our missions were of counterinsurgency nature in Laos and North Vietnam. There were about eight to ten CH-3Cs assigned to our unit at Udorn. They were not equipped with armor as were the *Jollys*. Since our mission was supposed to be clandestine, we just wanted all the weight/power ratio we could get. The only firepower we had initially were the crewmembers' weapons, usually M-16s. The aircraft were equipped with the original winch/hoist with 100 feet of cable. We retained the FOD deflector shield in front of the engines, and did not carry auxiliary fuel tanks.

In late 1967 the helicopters were upgraded to CH-3Es with more powerful 1,500hp engines. About half the pilots at that time were ex-school IPs (Instructor Pilots), and the rest were conversion pilots from other aircraft types. In the spring of 1968, some dumbass at headquarters decided we should have machine guns on our unarmored helicopters. The helicopters were equipped with a mount for an M-60 at the cabin door. As far as we were concerned it was in the way, and just extra weight. Our mission was to do it quietly and not make a lot of noise.

*Wearing black clothing, SOG team leader John Gilreath after being picked up by a Green Hornet Slick. (Tom Garcia)*

*The "Hornet's Nest" at Nha Trang. (James Bedingfield)*

# Green Hornets: The History of the U.S. Air Force 20th Special Operations Squadron

South Vietnamese Kingbee pilots were known for their daring, often paying a heavy price. This Kingbee H-34 barely made it back to Kontum's FOB in 1966. (Tom Garcia)

Alfonse Torres displays the XM-174 40mm grenade launcher used by 20th SOS gunships beginning in 1970. (Rich Jalloway)

Missions were flown with two helicopters, a high and low bird. The low bird would do the infiltration, while the high bird flew a ways off to act as decoy, and be there for rescue. There were usually a couple A-1s to cover us. The troops we carried were Laotian, Thai, and mercenary types indigenous to the area. There were numerous 'safe' sites, called 'Lima Sites' (LS), throughout Laos that were used for staging and refueling. Fuel was pumped from 55-gallon barrels using a hand pump, and many of the barrels were used by local inhabitants to build shelters. At LS 85, near Ban Cha Thao, in northern Laos, there was a TACAN station on top of a 5,000-foot karst mountain that was staffed by U.S. personnel; 20th helicopters brought supplies to the site. One of the favorite staging areas was LS 36 at Na Khang, which was 30 miles south of LS 85.

It had a good-sized runway and a military presence. A few times we retrieved downed aircraft."

The latter was an understatement in view of the 20th's involvement in one of the most unusual aviation incidents of the war. Since the top secret radar/TACAN site LS 85 atop Phou Pha Thi Mountain, in northern Laos, facilitated air strikes against North Vietnam, and was only 160 miles from Hanoi, a concerted effort by the North to destroy it was inevitable. The first strike came on 12 January 1968 when four Soviet-built Antonov AN-2 "Colt" biplanes of the North Vietnamese Air Force approached. Two of the Colts dropped mortar rounds and raked the site with gunfire and rockets, but were largely ineffective. An Air America Huey caught

Pony Express pilot Kyron Hall (right) and his copilot pose with Black Mariah prior to infiltrating a SOG road-watch team in Laos in 1967. (Alton Deviney)

A Pony Express CH-3 flies at treetop level prior to inserting a SOG team in 1968. Crewmen are armed with M-16s. Visible on the aft fuselage is a frame for easily removable national insignia. (Kyron Hall)

## Chapter 3: Into the Mouth of the Cat

Just five weeks after it arrived in Vietnam, on 17 June 1970, this UH-1P (s/n 64-15484) crashed and burned trying to avoid a collision with a CH-34. Two crewmen were killed, and the other two injured. Number 484 is seen here with "AO" tail code while assigned to the 317th SOS, 1st SOW at Hurlburt Field, Florida, in early 1970. (U.S. Air Force)

up with the pair, and its crew chief, firing a sub-machinegun from the doorway, scored hits on both Colts. One crashed and burned, and the other limped 12 miles from the site and crashed while trying to clear a ridge line less than one mile from the North Vietnamese border. Pony Express CH-3s participated in recovering the wreckage of that AN-2. Attacks on LS 85 continued, and on 11 March it was overrun by a sapper force, which killed or captured 11 of the 19 men manning the site. This was the largest single ground combat loss of USAF personnel during the war.

By the end of 1967, Green Hornet aircrew and SOG team members had proven that whatever disparity existed between the services in Washington did not affect their close working relationship in the field. Nevertheless, during early 1968 the position of Deputy Commander for Special Operations was created to help close the distance between the commands of Army SF and the 14th Special Operations Wing (SOW). A former Green Hornet notes:

"By July 1968 our camp was in pretty good shape. We had progressed from a tent city to wooden structures. Despite the segregation normally experienced in the military between ranks, we generally shared everything except sleeping quarters. It is no wonder the Green Hornets and Green Berets developed a close affinity for each other. Given this daily contact, you either distanced yourselves or you became close. We became close."

Special Forces member Keith Larson adds:

"The only reason we went where we did is that we knew they'd always come get us. It didn't matter how nasty it was. They had their testicles attached directly to their spines. Good people!"

Normally at least eight Green Hornet Hueys were allotted daily to Special Forces. A two-aircraft contingent was based at Tan Son Nhut Air Base to support Headquarters, 7th Air Force. A crew, usually consisting of a pilot and crew chief, flew classified film courier service in the Saigon area, and provided VIP transport. The Hueys were unarmed, and outfitted with seats in the cargo compartment. Personnel manning included a commander assigned for three months, and three pilots assigned for one month each. This assignment not only enabled inexperienced pilots to amass flying time, it also afforded the older hands a respite from combat.

A VNAF H-34 Kingbee on alert at Duc Lap in September 1970. Kingbees wore even less markings than Green Hornet Hueys. (James Green)

*Green Hornets: The History of the U.S. Air Force 20th Special Operations Squadron*

A UH-1F Slick mounting rope ladders in 1970. Serial number 65-7948 survived the war; more than half of the total number of UH-1F/P models flown by the 20th SOS did not. (James Green)

Although tactics varied according to lessons learned, and to fit each Green Hornet-SOG mission, seldom did they deviate from a basic tactical concept. SOG missions were usually planned for several weeks. One or two days before the mission, the SF team leader and a helicopter crew flew over the insertion site, taking photographs and selecting primary and alternate LZs, being sure to cover a broad area to avoid tipping their hand to the watching enemy.

Early on the day the mission was launched, the helicopters flew from the Forward Operating Base (FOB), usually Ban Me Thuot or Kontum, to a Forward Operating Location (FOL). These *alert strips* were Duc Lap, Duc Co, Ban Don, and Thieu Atar. Others from which missions were launched included Cheo Reo, LZ English, and in late 1970, An Loc and Da Nang.

SOG teams usually were inserted at twilight so they could slink into their mission area under the cover of darkness. The Special Forces officer in charge of the mission, who used the call sign "Padlock," flew overhead in an O-1, O-2, or OV-10 FAC aircraft. He was linked by radio with all the players, who were the SOG team and the helicopter force, which comprised any combination of Green Hornet slicks and gunships.

It quickly became apparent that the best way to get a team into an LZ was for the slick to go in very low and very fast. Although

Since Green Hornet missions normally were high drama, the unit's awards and decorations personnel were kept busy. Lt. Col. Harmon Brotnov presents 20th SOS gunner TSGT James Green with his second Distinguished Flying Cross on 16 May 1971. Green received the award for his part in saving a long-range recon team on 4 January that year. Green's first DFC was awarded for a similar mission on 20 October 1970. On both missions the gunship crews closed with large enemy forces, engaging in fierce battle to draw enemy fire from the teams. (U.S. Air Force)

One form of initiating new crewmen involved suspending them inverted from a Huey's tail "stinger," and setting off multiple smoke grenades. (James R. Wagner)

## Chapter 3: Into the Mouth of the Cat

Green Hornet personnel used this Christmas card with a tongue-in-cheek message for the 1971 holiday. (James R. Wagner)

the enemy could hear the choppers, it was difficult to get a fix on them and get a good shot. Since pilots skimming the treetops at 125 mph couldn't navigate toward the LZ, they relied implicitly on a *high bird* flying at about 2,000 feet to talk them in. Tom Garcia continues:

"Out of the danger of most small arms fire, and with an excellent view of things, the high bird radio conversation would sound like this: 'Looking good. Hold your present heading. That little hill ahead—either pop over the top of it or skirt around the left side.

Turn five degrees to the right, about two klicks (kilometers) to go now—okay, hold that heading. You are lined up just right.

One klick out now. Start slowing down—you're just about to cross an open area, and your LZ is the clearing beyond. Start your flare. A hundred meters now—honk it back—roll over and drop it in. That's the LZ right in front of you.'

The helicopter would drop down into the grass and hold a hover just a foot or two above the ground. If the terrain was uneven, which was often the case, just the tip of one skid might touch down. In 10 to 15 seconds the troops were out and gone, racing for the trees. The pilot was busy flying, so the copilot twisted around in his seat to watch the team leave, and he would punch the pilot in the arm as soon as it was time to lift off.

Departure from the area was done low, gathering speed, followed by a sharp pull-up to get out of range of ground fire. Sometimes another helicopter formation made a fake insertion a half mile away to trick the bad guys into thinking that two teams were on the ground. Another deception at the fake LZ involved staging

Obviously, at some point during its travels throughout Southeast Asia, this C-7 Caribou parked in the vicinity of Green Hornet aircrew. (James R. Wagner)

This Kingbee's catch, which was the result of flying low level and spotting a herd of deer, meant a hearty meal at the Forward Operating Base. (Tom Kreidler)

# Green Hornets: The History of the U.S. Air Force 20th Special Operations Squadron

Green Hornet and Kingbee crews on alert at Duc Lap in 1970. Jim Green explains: "We launched from BMT at first light, test-fired our guns over a river, then hot-refueled at the alert site. Ammo was topped off and rockets loaded. We carried the cots, water, and other items in the baggage compartment. On word to launch, it was amazing how fast we could put it all away, suit up, and go." (James Green)

a sham firefight with plenty of sound effects to add to the confusion.

Next came a period of high anxiety for the mission control officer. Was the team on the ground in good shape? Would they be able to move out of the LZ area and leave a cold enough trail so they could complete their mission? The first hour would tell the story. Just in case, the helicopters orbited 10 or 15 miles away for 20 minutes, and then headed back to base. The gunships in particular were restricted by their fuel load as to how long they could hang around. The idea behind limiting the fuel in the gunships was less gas and more ammo, up to a certain point."

Sometimes the answer as to the success of the mission came quickly. The slick crew, after going up to altitude following the drop-off, sometimes heard from Padlock, "Stick around. The team is in trouble."

A typical insertion mission had one or two slicks, protected by two to four gunships. An additional slick, with an SF medic on board, stayed high and a few miles west of the LZ. Later in the war, two gunships joined the extra slick as backup.

Amazingly, the five people aboard this UH-1P survived their injuries when they were shot down during gunnery training on 29 July 1970. (Gene L. Cole)

The North Vietnamese flag displayed by these Green Hornet crewmen was the target of a risky, self-imposed mission in fall 1968. A group of 20th SOS airmen agreed the flag would have to be removed from their free-fire zone near Nha Trang. A crew hovered and attempted to snatch the flag with a makeshift grappling hook, being careful not to trip a booby trap. Although the snatch was successful, the next day all involved were "standing tall" in front of an unhappy squadron commander. Darwin Edwards (kneeling) retained possession of the flag. (Robert Hill Collection)

## Chapter 3: Into the Mouth of the Cat

Swatting the hornet emblem on the tail boom of UH-1P s/n 65-7935 was a caricature associated with Air Force HH-43 "Pedro" rescue helicopters. Number 935 was lost on 8 December 1969. (Darwin Edwards)

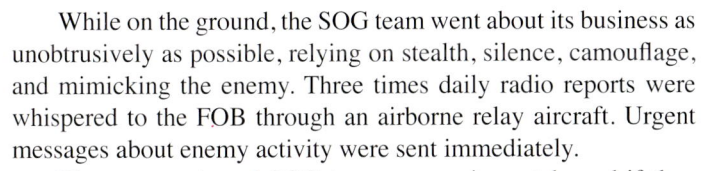

This AN-2 Colt of the North Vietnamese Air Force was shot down by an Air America crewman when it attacked TACAN site LS-85 in northern Laos on 12 January 1968. Pony Express CH-3s were involved with its recovery to LS-36 at Na Khang. Much of the Colt's fabric was removed by local tribesmen, and the code "665-C" on the tail fin became an Air America or USAF crewman's souvenir. (Official DoD photo via LTC Geoff Hays, USAFR, Ret.)

While on the ground, the SOG team went about its business as unobtrusively as possible, relying on stealth, silence, camouflage, and mimicking the enemy. Three times daily radio reports were whispered to the FOB through an airborne relay aircraft. Urgent messages about enemy activity were sent immediately.

The enemy viewed SOG teams as a prize catch, and if they discovered one in their backyard, they stopped at nothing to capture or destroy it. As many soldiers as possible were brought in for the hunt. Often, the enemy preferred surrounding the team and using it as bait for the rescue force they knew would come. A team on the run had nothing to lose. With the enemy in hot pursuit, the team's goal was to head for the closest LZ, under the guidance of its FAC.

An extraction's level of difficulty depended mainly upon the weather, terrain, and enemy situation. If a team was too far from an LZ, or none was available, helicopter crewmen could drop a McGuire rig, which incorporated a rope loop and canvas seat. A Huey carried four rigs, which were attached to 120-foot ropes. Later came the STABO rig, which was not only safer, but allowed the commandos' arms to be free to latch onto each other while "riding the strings," or to fire their weapons during the snatch from the enemy's reach. Slicks also mounted flexible 30-foot ladders similar to those used by the Army to haul troops aboard CH-47 "Chinook" helicopters. Although called a "rope" ladder, the device was made of aluminum rungs and aircraft cable.

The helicopter extraction force typically comprised five Hueys. Two gunships, labeled "Hornet One" and "Two," were the primary alert choppers, along with "Hornet Five" as the slick. "Hornets Three" and "Four" were backup gunships, and launched 15 to 20 minutes after the first three. The FAC called the launch, often marking the LZ with a smoke rocket, while informing Hornet crews where precisely the team and the enemy were located.

Besides high-risk SOG missions, Pony Express crews kept busy searching for downed fliers, hauling equipment, and recovering aircraft. Here, CH-3B s/n 65-5691 prepares to lift a battered Marine UH-1E of VMO-6 at Hep Duc in 1968. Number 691 was shot down in Laos on 27 June 1969. (Ed Alexander)

## Green Hornets: The History of the U.S. Air Force 20th Special Operations Squadron

A 20th SOS CH-3 recovers a Skyraider of the 602nd SOS after it was fired upon and crash-landed in Thailand in March 1968. (Kyron Hall Collection)

Its camouflage blending well with its surroundings, a Pony Express CH-3E rides the current of the Mekong River in April 1968. Serial number 62-12579 was destroyed by ground fire in Laos the following year. (Kyron Hall)

Knowing the exact position of everyone on the ground was vital, since the SOG team commonly dressed like the enemy. When the team was pinpointed, the gunships dove for the treetops and set up a protective ring of fire. Time on target for the gunships was no more than 15 minutes, or when they ran out of ammunition. If the slick had not yet snatched the team, Hornet One and Two headed back to rearm and refuel, and Hornets Three and Four rolled in to provide continuous fire.

This rotation continued until the arrival of A-1 Skyraiders, whose pilots were accustomed to SOG support. Likewise, team members were expert at calling in air strikes, usually marking their position with smoke and a colored panel. That SOG teams called in bombing runs just yards from their position, sometimes at the cost of being wounded, said much about their confidence in A-1 pilots.

Team extractions after dark had been attempted on occasion, but were extremely dangerous and largely unsuccessful, even with the assistance of flare ships. In one incident, on 3 April 1968, Green Hornet crews were scrambled to assist a SOG team under attack. As darkness approached, gunships laid down protective fire while Major Norman Eldridge searched in vain for an LZ. Having no intention of leaving the team on the ground, Eldridge found an opening in the jungle canopy, lowered a rope ladder, and hovered with his aircraft lights on, while the team scrambled up the ladder. The FAC called off extraction attempts if the team could not be pulled out by dark. Tactical air support, usually in the form of AC-47, AC-119, or AC-130 gunships, was available to support the team throughout the night.

By the end of 1967, SOG teams had worn thin their element of surprise. As the action increased, so too did Green Hornet losses. Five Hueys were lost—four to enemy fire—during 1967 and 1968. During a mission on 19 February 1968, a UH-1F was shot down attempting a team rescue. The demands of the mission produced battle fatigue to the extent that 20th pilots were rotated weekly.

Special Forces soldiers prepare to board number 579 for a parachute jump at Camp Honke in southern Thailand in May 1968. (Kyron Hall)

## Chapter 3: Into the Mouth of the Cat

Crew chiefs and gunners did not rotate as often, the crew chief staying with his aircraft until it went to the main support base for the 100-hour maintenance *phase*. Hueys often did not make it to the 100-hour mark. The red laterite dust of Vietnam's central highlands proved injurious to the Huey's power plant, resulting in frequent engine changes. Due to the absence of an adequate air inlet filtering system, the abrasive dust injected into the engine eroded its first two power-producing stages. Before an efficient inlet filtering system was introduced, engines were changed every 80 to 100 hours, compared with 300 to 600 hours of normal operation between engine replacements.

From a maintenance standpoint, the 20th was also hindered by a shortage of experienced helicopter mechanics. The majority of senior maintenance personnel had converted from fixed-wing aircraft, and most of the maintenance section was made up of young semi-trained airmen. Jim Pedriana, who served as a 20th crew chief in 1969, comments:

"The crew chief was also a weapons specialist. This was an interchangeable position—left or right side of the aircraft. The pilot/aircraft commander flew right seat."

Kingbees stand alert at Thieu Atar in January 1971. (James Green)

Pony Express had the awesome responsibility of re-supplying TACAN sites, which were at extreme elevations. Here a 20th SOS CH-3 is perched atop the 5,000-foot elevation Channel 72 site in Laos in 1968. (Kyron Hall)

## Green Hornets: The History of the U.S. Air Force 20th Special Operations Squadron

David Sparks has this to say about crew positions:

"The majority of the pilots assigned to the squadron in 1969 were fixed-wing conversion pilots with less than 100 hours of first pilot helicopter time. Sprinkled in, fortunately, were some old experienced chopper pilots with excellent backgrounds to perform instructor pilot duties and stan/eval (standardization/evaluation) work.

As for gunners, the young men we had assigned were eager and willing to learn how to shoot the guns. There was much more to their part of the mission than shooting. They had to be capable of giving precise directions to the pilot while descending into jungle landing zones. This they learned well."

Skip Cantwell explains the path he took to becoming a Green Hornet:

"In 1970 the Air Force called for volunteers for *Operation Palace Gun*. This was a plan to find qualified 462s (TAC aircraft weapon mechanics) to undergo training to become airborne gunners on AC-47, AC-119, and AC-130 gunships in Southeast Asia. At the time there was no mention of helicopters. I received my orders right away.

Special Forces soldiers practice rope ladder extraction with a 20th SOS CH-3. (Kyron Hall)

One method of extracting SOG men involved the use of 120-foot ropes attached to McGuire rigs. Commandos have been lost, or severely injured "riding the strings." (Kyron Hall)

The first thing after passing the flight physical was attending the Air Force Physiological Training (altitude chamber). For me this meant a short TDY to the 93rd Bombardment Wing at Castle AFB, California, in March 1970. The next stop was the USAF Survival School at Fairchild AFB, Spokane, Washington. After that it was on to the Special Operations Force Course, UH-1N Gunner (SEA). This was given by the 317th SOS (TAC), 1st SOW at Eglin AFB, Florida. I then reported to the PACAF Jungle Survival School in the Philippines. Once done with the jungle school, it was off to Vietnam. I arrived at Cam Ranh Bay, RVN, around the 20th of January 1971, and signed in to the 20th SOS." Cantwell adds, "Because I went into Army SF shortly afterward, I have a good deal of knowledge of the SF side of the operations."

By 1971 the 20th SOS had categorized aircrew positions according to the following qualifications: Gun Mission Qualified, Slick Mission Qualified, Gunship Instructor Gunner, Slick Instructor Gunner, Gunship Flight Examiner, and Slick Flight Examiner.

David Galvan describes a disturbing aspect of having been a Green Hornet crew chief:

"As gunners, we had a moral dilemma to wrestle with on every hot exfiltration. We were briefed by the teams that if they were captured, and we could see them, we were to kill them. We were also briefed that only the same number of people dropped off days earlier would be picked up. If we dropped off eleven, we were to shoot a twelfth, or more persons trying to join the team. Thankfully, I never had to deal with either situation."

On a similar note, which underscores the seriousness of such work, it was understood by both Green Hornet aircrew and SOG teams that if men were *riding the strings* out of a hot area, and the aircraft became disabled, the ropes would be cut to save the aircraft.

## Chapter 3: Into the Mouth of the Cat

Both of the Pony Express CH-3Es (s/n 64-14236, at left; and 64-14237), seen here at a refueling site in Laos, were lost in action. (Kyron Hall)

"In addition to personal weapons," Galvan says, "I wore a web belt with two water canteens, a loaded pistol, spare ammo, an emergency radio, two spare batteries, and a survival knife. I wore an armored chest protector, and a gunner's restraint (nylon webbing to prevent being thrown out), which was clipped to tie-down rings.

Enroute to the target we flew at 5,000 feet. When we went in, it was at treetop level, with gunners calling the targets by clock positions through the turns. The pilot flew the aircraft, avoiding branches larger than a person's wrist. The copilot watched the instruments. Many a good pilot fell to temptation and scanned the instruments, and hit trees. We flew directly over the good guys, and saturated everything else with the miniguns at 2,000spm—4,000spm was reserved for someone shooting at you. When the slick went down to pick up the team, the two gunships continued firing as they passed over the slick and the team. We then escorted the slick, between the two gunships, at treetop level, the first gun firing forward, and the other firing under the slick, while we climbed to a safe altitude."

Jim Burns has this to say about extractions:

"One of the SOG teams I supported was led by Jerry 'Mad Dog' Shriver. He is a legend in SOG, and went MIA in 1969. We knew that any time Shriver was in the field, we could expect to make the extraction under fire. I remember one time that he and his team were on the run, and had gone into a huge bamboo thicket. He told me that the bad guys did not like to chase them into bam-

Using colored panels and smoke, a SOG team signals a 20th HS CH-3 for pickup in December 1967. (Kyron Hall)

Underscoring the hazard of flying in Laos, this 21st SOS CH-3 was flying at nearly 10,000 feet in 1969 when a 37mm shell entered the rear cargo ramp opening and exited the fuselage. Had the CH-3E's rear ramp not been removed to lighten the aircraft, the outcome may have been more disastrous. (James Burns)

# Green Hornets: The History of the U.S. Air Force 20th Special Operations Squadron

Taken from atop a crashed CH-3E, this photo captures Black Mariah and two sister CH-3s high atop LS-85 in December 1967. (Kyron Hall)

Evident here is the variety of "spook" aircraft that frequented Lima sites in Laos. Seen here at LS-36 in March 1968 are, from left, a CH-53, an Air America Pilatus Porter, an Air America DHC-4 Caribou, a CH-3, a CH-34, and an Air America Huey. None of these aircraft wore markings identifying their nationality. Fuel drums and their lids were strewn across the parking area. (Kyron Hall)

UH-1Ps and UH-1Ns stand alert at Tuy Hoa in August 1970. (James Green)

## Chapter 3: Into the Mouth of the Cat

Serial number 63-13163 was one of the last Hueys to serve the squadron. It is seen here at Cam Ranh Bay, the last Green Hornets' duty station, in 1971, wearing an alternate camouflage pattern of tan and medium green. (Tom Hansen)

A UH-1N of the 1st SOW at Hurlburt Field was used for rappelling training in late 1971. (Dwayne Meyer)

boo. We were able to get down low enough to get them in on a rope ladder, however, it was real close, and we were chopping the tops off the bamboo. As we left the area with them on board, we hit a large stand of bamboo, and the bird picked up a severe vibration. It was so bad that we told the gunships to find us a clearing to set down as soon as possible. They found a clear area a short distance away, and we set it down. We looked at the blades, discovering that the tab on one had been bent. We straightened the tab, and after three or four tries, we were able to get the blade tracked smooth enough to fly us back to camp. It seemed odd that on a prior mission we had damaged a blade so badly after striking tree limbs that it had to be replaced, yet the bird flew smoothly."

As with all units involved with supporting special operations, teamwork and routine acts of heroism were commonplace. Not only was pilot James Fleming awarded the Medal of Honor for rescuing a seven-man patrol on 26 November 1968, the day before he had rescued a SOG team that a large enemy force had trapped in an open field with a river at its back. Leonard Gonzales, whose gunship was shot down during Fleming's MOH mission, explains:

"On the day previous, Fleming received the Silver Star. The mission was very hairy, because I had to hover my gunship between the slick and the North Vietnamese force, which was right behind the SF team racing at full speed to reach the rescue helicopter. The grass was very high, and the wind from the blades of the gunship blew the grass down, exposing the North Vietnamese soldiers, who were very close to the team. The minigun fire from my gunners enabled the team to board the slick without losing a team member."

On 27 November, the day after his MOH mission, Fleming flew as copilot on a mission that earned a crew chief the Air Force Cross. Gonzales begins:

SOG commandos on the strings of a UH-1N in 1971. (James R. Wagner)

41

# Green Hornets: The History of the U.S. Air Force 20th Special Operations Squadron

A SOG team prepares for one of the last missions of the Green Hornets' existence in 1972. (Fred McGuire)

"As we were inserting a team near Duc Co, the slick was shot down below me as it was preparing to land. The helicopter landed upside down and burned. We lost most of the Special Forces team with the exception of the team leader, who was pulled out of the burning helicopter by TSGT Victor R. Adams, who was awarded the Air Force Cross. This was the first time we had lost a member of the Special Forces."

The mission was to infiltrate a six-man SOG team into an enemy bivouac area at Phu Nai, Cambodia. Flying the slick carrying the team, Captain William Dyer began a high steep approach into a ravine surrounded by high jungle. Enemy gunfire ripped into the Huey's controls, causing it to crash, roll over, and burst into flames. Of the ten souls aboard, five survived. Both pilots, gunner Adams, and two team members escaped, one of whom was rescued by Adams. The crew chief, SSGT Gene P. Stuifbergen, was trapped in the wreckage, becoming the first Green Hornet enlisted member lost in combat. The backup slick was able to land and rescue the survivors. Gonzales recalls:

"On another mission we landed an SF team in the middle of a resting North Vietnamese unit. All hell broke loose. We had to stay on top of the team, making tight 360-degree turns, and provide gunfire support to enable a rescue helicopter to pull the team out.
One of the missions that sticks out in my mind was when an SF team leader was seriously wounded, and told his team to leave him. When that was relayed to us we replied that we would stay as long as needed. We pulled back on our power, and stayed there until the team was able to carry him to a small clearing made by a bomb burst."

## 1969

Special operations support peaked during 1969, but it was not the best of times for the 20th SOS. Trouble started early in the year with the loss of a Huey on 3 January. During a second attempt to rescue a SOG team in Cambodia, the UH-1F was shot down, killing gunner SGT Ronald P. Zenga. David Sparks provides more insight:

"As the year progressed, many factors entered the picture concerning the destiny of the 20th and its personnel: newly converted helicopter pilots being assigned, engine failures causing many crashes, and the loss of our commander and DSCO in a fatal crash in March. Our move from Nha Trang to Tuy Hoa was demoralizing for all of us; we couldn't believe that if our mission was so important, we could be moved off like an unwanted stepchild. Tuy Hoa facilities were not ready for us in September. All these factors caused morale to fade. The mission suffered. We couldn't support it for a time after the Tuy Hoa move. Confidence in the UH-1P was down. The indifference of the 7th Air Force to our problems (until we became the focus of attention due to crashes) made 1969 a tough year."

Meanwhile, the Thailand-based element of the 20th SOS (the Pony Express) in January evacuated more than 5,000 villagers in northern Laos, where the enemy took over the region. The six-day

A flight of UH-1Ns enroute to a mission area in August 1971. (James R. Wagner)

42

## Chapter 3: Into the Mouth of the Cat

operation tested the mettle of CH-3 crews, who flew in fog over enemy controlled mountainous terrain. Tempering the mission's success was the loss on 17 January of a CH-3 while supplying a TACAN site in northern Laos. Three crew members and three passengers died in the crash.

As the North Vietnamese honed their skills in the now familiar hunt for SOG teams, Green Hornet Hueys fell to enemy gunners. On 13 February eight Hueys launched to rescue a team that was surrounded and trading blows with the enemy. While five Hueys orbited out of range, a slick, along with two covering gunships, dashed in for the rescue. The slick was hit and caught fire. The pilot was able to make a controlled landing into dense trees. As the backup slick hovered over the downed crew with rope ladders dangling, SGT Isidro Arroyo helped his wounded copilot up the ladder. As Arroyo began losing his grip on the man, who went into shock and began struggling, the slick lowered the pair into a tree so he could get a better grip to complete the climb into the chopper.

Two months later, Arroyo again would distinguish himself in combat. On 13 April the enemy fired on a flight of Green Hornet Hueys that had just pulled out a SOG team. A gunship was hit, killing its pilot, Captain James O. Lynch. The aircraft commander, although seriously wounded, managed to land the Huey in a clearing, snapping its tail boom and tearing off its skids. Despite back wounds, Arroyo carried the wounded pilot and the dead copilot to a slick that had turned back to get them. Since the slick was already overloaded, Arroyo waited on the ground for another chopper to pick him up. While moving the pilots, the gunner had removed vital equipment from the gunship, which was destroyed to prevent it from falling into enemy hands. For his selfless actions during both shoot-downs, Arroyo received the 1969 Cheney Award.

The XM-93 system left little room in the UH-1P's cabin for anything other than two gunners. Ammunition was belt-fed from magazines fastened to the cabin's aft bulkhead. (General Electric)

Even before the end of the first quarter of 1969, the action and subsequent losses continued. On 26 March, a Green Hornet slick flying at 4,000 feet near Duc My, South Vietnam, was believed to be hit by ground fire. When a severe vibration began, the pilot began an auto-rotation; however, the main rotor head came apart, and the rotors severed the tail boom. Seven men died in the crash. They were: Lt. Col. Frank A. DiFiglia, the pilot and commanding officer of the 20th SOS; copilot Capt. Walter C. Booth, who was the squadron maintenance officer; crew chief TSGT Jesse C. Bowman; gunner SGT Antonio L. Alho; Capt. Robert W. Fields, the 20th's flight surgeon; and Colonels Donald G. LePard and J.B. Levesque, both of Headquarters, 14th SOW. Dale L. Eppinger notes:

"I arrived in Southeast Asia in late June 1968, and had a one-year tour flying slicks. Unfortunately, I was on every mission during that 12-month period when we lost helicopters to ground fire-five in all. I was *flight lead* on Jim Fleming's MOH mission. My aircraft and crew were shot down on 21 April 1969 in Cambodia while extracting a seven-man Special Forces team. I received an Air Force Cross, and both of my gunners received Silver Stars."

Crew-operated GAU-2B/A miniguns and LAU-59/A rocket launchers were the muscle of 20th SOS gunships. The flex chute attached to the minigun carried spent cartridges safely below the aircraft. (James R. Wagner)

On this mission, Eppinger rushed to aid the team when they came under heavy fire. The team reported that they were out of wa-

# Green Hornets: The History of the U.S. Air Force 20th Special Operations Squadron

A SOG team rides the strings of a UH-1N out of a hot area in 1971. At the first sign of a clearing in a secure area, the chopper landed to bring the team aboard. (James R. Wagner)

Kingbee H-34s fly formation with Green Hornet UH-1Ns in 1971. (James R. Wagner)

ter, dehydrated, and exhausted. After numerous rounds of working over the area, and returning to re-arm and re-fuel, it was decided to attempt an extraction. With a gunship leading and firing rockets, Eppinger and three gunships followed. When he was 20 feet above the LZ gunfire erupted, wounding his onboard medic. Eppinger settled into the LZ, and the team scrambled aboard. Amid the confusion common in the din of battle, a gunner told Eppinger to lift out of the LZ. Eppinger picks up the story:

"At about 40 to 50 feet of altitude the right gunner came back on interphone and said, 'There's one American on the ladder and one on the ground.' I immediately stopped the aircraft and backed down to reposition over the LZ. Just as I was about to descend vertically, there was another burst of automatic weapons fire, and the engine immediately seized. I accomplished a hovering autorotation from about 12 feet above the ground, nearly missing the two Americans."

Since the ground team was completely exhausted, Eppinger took control of the situation, setting up security and directing Army Cobra gunships and Green Hornet gunships, who placed ordnance within 50 meters of his position. "Wave after wave of Cobras provided outstanding support with both minigun and 40mm fire," says Eppinger. Almost seven hours into the battle, the FAC informed him that three Army OH-6A "Loaches" were inbound to pick them up. Two of the Loaches were able to land, under fire, to rescue everyone on the ground. Summarizing the battle, Eppinger says:

"The Cobra support, and the 20th support were outstanding. To the Loach pilots we owe our lives."

Across the fence, combat operations kept Pony Express crews equally busy. In early March, two of the Thailand-based UH-1Fs were diverted from support of a communications site to help the two-man crew of an Army OV-1 Mohawk shot down in southern Laos. Guided by a second OV-1, the Huey crews braved small arms and 12.7mm fire to rescue the Army pilots.

The 20th's sister CH-3 unit in Thailand, the 21st SOS, had some of its CH-3s modified with Emerson Electric TAT-102B 7.62mm miniguns. A sponson housed the gun and 8,000 rounds of ammunition. The system was phased out by 1971, since the weapon could not be repaired in flight. This CH-3E (s/n 66-13295) was the Dustdevil's first combat loss of the war, having gone down on 23 May 1968, killing all five crewmen. (U.S. Air Force)

# Chapter 3: Into the Mouth of the Cat

Robert Steinbrunn, an Army Huey pilot during the war, photographed UH-1F s/n 64-15491. He notes: "This was taken at BMT in April 1968 during heavy fighting west of there. I was flying a UH-1C with A Troop, 7th Squadron, 17th Air Cavalry, and took over 40 hits in my ship."

Later that month three 20th pilots were wounded, and four helicopters received battle damage while extracting a 230-man assault force. One month later, Pony Express CH-3Es and UH-1Fs, protected by eight Skyraiders, inserted a large assault force while under enemy fire. By mid 1969, the number of missions into Cambodia decreased sharply, with 20th duties shifting to the support of VNAF H-34s operating in Cambodia.

Adding to the squadron's woes in 1969 was the grounding of the Huey fleet for one month following the loss of three Hueys due to engine failures. The squadron's relocation to cramped quarters at Tuy Hoa only made matters worse. After the move, aircraft and crews working out of Ban Me Thuot were called "B Flight."

## The 21st SOS

The 20th's CH-3 element in Thailand, the Pony Express, was experiencing its own share of problems while merging with the CH-3-equipped 21st SOS. The unit—whose members called themselves the "Dustdevils," and used the call sign "Knife"—was activated at NKP to expand the capabilities of the 56th SOW. Former 21st pilot Robert Arnau points out:

"The 21st was originally formed, and began training in 1967 for the specific role of dropping sensors in Laos in support of *Igloo White*, 'McNamara's Line.' In 1968 the 21st suffered very heavy losses of CH-3s, and the sensor mission was soon transferred to the more suitable F-4C fighters. The 21st then picked up a new role of supporting SOG teams in Laos, and joined the *Ponies* in supporting the Air Force DOSA (Director of Operations for Special Activities) mission."

Although merging the 20th into the 21st to consolidate all CH-3 assets in Thailand seemed a good idea, many Pony Express members felt that their unit did not die an honorable death. Discord at the wing level created infighting, which only worsened with the realization that the mission load remained disproportionate. Compared to the larger NKP-based 21st Helicopter Squadron, the 20th's D Flight at Udorn had only nine CH-3s to handle their primary twofold mission of TACAN site support, and clandestine operations for the DOSA.

Trouble started when the commander of the 56th SOW proposed that the 20th move to NKP. A bitter compromise had three aircraft relocated there, with the remaining six left at the Udorn FOL. Many felt that the wing commander's unsuccessful attempt to move the entire unit to NKP sparked his personal campaign of eradicating the remnants of the Pony Express. Anything that hinted "Pony Express" was ordered removed. The tenseness of the situation became pervasive. The contingent at Udorn defiantly grew moustaches, and touted their Pony label. More importantly, they preserved their heritage by flying more combat time during the last three months of 1969 than the entire NKP-based unit, and with only four available aircraft.

As an example of how special operations helicopter tactics were developed during the war, two CH-3E *Knife* pilots provide the following. John Holt explains:

"When I first started flying Prairie Fire missions, the procedure was that both helicopters descend very low. *Knife 52* would usually be at about 100 to 200 feet circling *Knife 51*. After one or two missions I decided that was stupid, as a gun could shoot us both down. After that I had Knife 52 stay near 5,000 feet while I dropped off the team. When I was shot down I clearly remember telling Knife 52 to keep his eyes on me, as we would be difficult to see after we went into the trees. We had no stripe on our rotors. I remember Knife 52 saying during our descent into the trees, 'I've lost you John!' That frightened me as much as the guns."

Robert Arnau adds:

"On Prairie Fire missions one CH-3E (Knife 51) went low to infil/exfil the team, while Knife 52 and 53 remained in a high orbit, prepared to come in if needed. From above it was very difficult to see the camouflaged helicopter over the jungle. To solve the problem, a wide white stripe was painted across the top of one of the five rotor blades. That made it easier for the high helicopters, A-1 escorts, and *Nail* FAC to keep the low/lead in sight, without making sighting easier for the bad guys on the ground. I believe the *Jollys* used the stripe as well."

Arnau recounts a memorable mission he flew as a Knife CH-3E pilot. His copilot was Jerry Kibby, and his two flight engineers (FEs) were Jim Burns and Charles Hill. The emergency exfil occurred on 18 November 1969.

"The SOG team had come into contact with the NVA close to 'The Trail' during the night, and was surrounded and under attack. Of the six team members, one had been killed, and two others were wounded. Unfortunately, the weather in the area was terrible; low clouds and visibility, and severe turbulence. We launched immediately from NKP with three CH-3s and two A-1 escorts. On arrival in the area we made contact with the NAIL FAC, who had a 'Heavy Hook' (SOG) rider with him. I was pleased to discover that the NAIL was 1/Lt. Hank Haden, an outstanding young FAC from NKP, with whom I had worked other emergency exfils.

Hank was below the overcast and, despite the fact the clouds were almost on the karst tops, was directing air strikes against the enemy. He advised us that the turbulence in the area was quite severe, and that our planned approach route to the team was not usable due to the low clouds. The good news was that there was a hole in the undercast that we could descend through. The bad news was that the hole was over a known 23mm gun. Obviously there was no choice, and we went through the hole. Once the formation was below the cloud layer, following standard tactics, the other two helicopters held clear while keeping us in sight as we followed the FAC into the team's location.

We spotted the team's smoke on a steep ridge line that was covered with tall, dense elephant grass. As we made our approach, the team remained under small arms and automatic weapon fire, and our escorting A-1s were delivering protective ordnance. The steep slope of the ridge prevented a landing, so we hovered with the nose wheel on the ground and the main gear in the air over the precipice. The wind turbulence coming over the edge of the ridge was indeed severe, and the CH-3 was bucking wildly as we hovered.

Despite the years that have elapsed, I clearly recall my initial glimpse of the team as they came into the area of elephant grass blown flat by the rotor downwash. The first two team members were dragging their dead comrade by his boots. With the helicopter bucking like a rodeo bull, the team had difficulty getting the body on board, and it seemed like an eternity before all were finally on board. The A-1s continued to lay down protective fire as we came safely off the ridge line.

After the exfil, we had the privilege of having a beer with the surviving team members at the SOG Heavy Hook compound at NKP. I asked the Heavy Hook commander, Major Bill Shelton, why, since they were under fire, didn't the team leave the body. He explained to me the importance to the Nungs/Vietnamese of returning the body of the team member to his home village for a proper Buddhist funeral. That the SOG Special Forces members would go to that extent—recovering the body while under fire, and managing to get it aboard a nearly out of control helicopter—to assure the loyalty and future support of their indigenous troops, made me respect them more than ever! Those guys were unbelievable!"

Jerry Kibby adds his view from "the other seat":

"The A-1s providing close air support were unable to work in their usual way. The low clouds and high terrain forced them to stay under the clouds, and they had to make long horizontal passes at the target, during which they strafed with 20mm cannons for much of the pass. After passing the target area, they had to remain under the clouds and fly a horizontal loop back to the target. While they were doing this, they had to avoid the high terrain, each other, and the two other CH-3s.

When we had the team on board, Bob turned us to face downhill, and we accelerated just above the ground level down the hill. We passed right over a gun position, which did not have time to come to bear on our aircraft. I also recall a sudden sickening feeling as we ran down the hill—smoke in the aircraft. Our FEs were putting out all the fire they could from our M-60s, and the CH-3's shape causes a reverse airflow, pulling air and gun smoke from the back up to the front and out the windows.

A Special Forces team member later told me that their wounded were injured by their own grenades, which they had to lay down to keep the enemy off of them. He also told me that our helicopter, as it sat with the nose gear on the karst to pick them up, was on top of some of the NVA surrounding them. I sure hope he made it through the rest of the war."

The merge with the 21st SOS, which took effect on 1 August, left the 20th an all-Huey squadron. The Thailand-based Hueys joined those at Nha Trang. During its time in Southeast Asia, the 20th was never authorized more than 21 UH-1 helicopters; however, seldom were more than 17 assigned. An even fewer number

Barely visible in this photo is a seven-man SOG team being extracted by CH-3 s/n 63-9681. This aircraft tempted fate by serving both the 20th SOS and 21st SOS, and was shot down in Laos in August 1970. (U.S. Air Force)

## Chapter 3: Into the Mouth of the Cat

were in operational readiness status, as the result of an erratic overhaul schedule, and a shortage of major aircraft components. The constant aircraft shortage and low in-commission rate meant that only one-third of the 39 assigned pilots were gun mission qualified.

**1970**

The year 1970 saw a number of improvements, including the reassignment of crew chiefs from the maintenance to operations section to ensure adequate crew rest. A crew chief and assistant crew chief were assigned to each aircraft, and both went with the Huey to the FOL. At home station the crew chief worked day shift, and the assistant worked night shift. When the pipeline for gunners dried up during early 1970, and helicopter mechanics became hard to find, the 7th Air Force solicited volunteers through a program called *Operation Palace Dog*.

Losses continued to plague the Green Hornets. On 14 March a UH-1P was shot down near Duc Lap while supporting a ground team. The pilot, Captain Dana A. Dilley, was killed, and the instructor pilot and both gunners were injured. Five days later another Huey was shot down during a two-ship training flight at Dar Lac, claiming the lives of both pilots, Captains Clyde W. Enderle and Carlos A. Estrada, Jr., and gunner TSGT James W. Greenwood. Gunner A1C John Visnesky was severely injured when he was thrown clear.

Early in the year, the XM-174 grenade launcher was introduced to the squadron. The hand-held 40mm weapon was yet another version of the popular 40mm launcher, which had already been proven as an aircraft turret and an infantry weapon. Jim Fudge describes a mission on which he was a gunner, and carried the XM-94:

"A team was in trouble and trying to make it to an LZ. Green Hornet lead took us down to the treetops, where we set up a racetrack pattern. My minigun jammed on the second pass right in front of the bad guys. The pucker factor was very high. Each gunner carried a spare gun feed assembly that we could use to repair our gun in flight. But you risked being shot down while you tried to work on the gun. With all the hostility shown by the bad guys that day, I figured that I had best resort to my backup weapon of the day, my 40mm automatic grenade launcher. It held 12 rounds in a canister, and could be fired single shot or automatic. I chose single shot, because I didn't want to run out of ammo too soon. Shooting the weapon from a moving aircraft was like throwing a baseball out the window of your car at 100 miles per hour and trying to hit a stop sign. It took a lot of practice to come even close to your target. I was hoping to make a lot of noise with the 40mm, and hopefully keep the bad guys' heads down long enough for us to do our job."

Since Fudge's right gunner fired all his minigun ammo, and they were taking hits, both aircraft pulled out of the fight, being replaced by two more Green Hornets. Fudge adds:

"On landing we discovered that we were in pretty bad shape. Armor piercing rounds had entered our fuel cells and left engine.

*This UH-1C gunship belonged to the 57th AHC, which was one of numerous Army helicopter units supporting SOG missions. The rocket and minigun armed Huey is seen hover-taxiing at Phu Cat Air Base in October 1970. (Norman E. Taylor)*

With our bird out of action, the pilot of *Hornet Lead* wounded, the other aircraft shot up, and daylight almost gone, we decided that our fight was over for the day. The FAC arranged for nighttime gunship support from the 16th SOS *Spectres* at Udorn, Thailand. The team was extracted the next morning by a team of Cobras and a Vietnamese Army slick crew. Just another day."

Besides the addition of XM-174s to the squadron inventory, more good news came in the form of replacement aircraft, five of which arrived during June. Two were shipped from Hurlburt Field and three from Howard AFB, Canal Zone. This brought the total assigned UH-1s to 20, 15 of which were operationally ready.

In 1970 the Green Hornets began providing support for Army slicks carrying Long Range Reconnaissance Patrols (LRRP). Most missions, however, were flown in support of VNAF H-34s, especially during the push into Cambodia. For these operations, Duc Lap became the 20th's Forward Operating Location, while vast improvements were made to the facilities at Ban Me Thuot. The effort to turn over more operations to the VNAF continued, with training conducted by the 20th personnel, and with Kingbees doing the actual team insertions. On 29 July a UH-1P was shot down while conducting gunnery training. Both pilots, along with the gunnery instructor and two student gunners, were injured. The aircraft was recovered, but was written off as a combat loss due to extensive damage.

On 25 September, the same day the 20th closed its doors at Tuy Hoa AB and moved to Cam Ranh Bay, another Green Hornet would be stricken from the inventory. David Galvan, the crew chief of UH-1P serial number 64-15484, tells how it happened:

"After flying to BMT we departed to Duc Lap. This was crew change day; new in, old out. As soon as we landed we got out of our gear, and the pilots went to the mission tent. It seemed like I had just gotten out of my gear when the pilots came out of the

47

# Green Hornets: The History of the U.S. Air Force 20th Special Operations Squadron

tent, one waving a hand over his head in a circular motion; we had a scramble. The other three crew members were Captain Jackie P. Heil, copilot Captain Henry B. Carrington, and MSGT Gerald A. Cooper. We were to escort Kingbee to re-supply a team that had been due to come out. There were no bad guys near the team, which was near an abandoned airfield at Mondol Kiri, Cambodia. As we neared the LZ, we dropped from 5,000 feet to treetop. There was a ridge between the LZ and us, with a saddle where we were to enter the LZ, for less exposure to ground fire. The mission should have been routine, since the team was sure there were no bad guys in the area. This being the case, the IP took the opportunity to explain all the scenarios to the new pilot. In the meantime, the first gunship and the Kingbee had entered the area to make the drop. There was also a FAC. Part of everyone's job was to monitor all the mission frequencies to be aware of each player's position and their situation. Unfortunately, in our aircraft we were distracted by the lesson the IP was giving, and we were lulled into a false sense of safety. The other aircraft had been trying to raise us to inform us that Kingbee was coming through the saddle after making the drop. It reached the point where everyone was shouting into their microphones to get our attention.

We were rapidly approaching the apex of the saddle, at about 100 knots, when we finally heard that Kingbee was approaching. The instant we reached the apex we saw the other chopper coming at us at the same speed. The new pilot instantly made a very sharp right bank, which most certainly saved us from a head-on. But we lost a lot of altitude, and as the pilot banked left, a tall dead tree took off our tail boom. With no tail rotor, a helicopter fuselage tends to rotate with the blades, unless you maintain airspeed above 70 knots. Pulling in collective to slow down descent, or climbing, would have caused fuselage spin. So we maintained our speed of 70 to 90 knots. We had to make a controlled descent through three levels of jungle. Having no rudder control, the pilot said, 'We're going in!' As we crashed down through the trees, my life did not flash before me, but everything seemed to be in slow motion, as I watched the trees wave back and forth as we plowed through them. It became darker and darker as we went deeper into the jungle.

I saw my minigun, with its beefy mounting system, ripped from the floor, while the rotor blades were sprinkling shreds of honeycombed aluminum as they were destroyed by trees. My thoughts changed from *this can't be happening* to *this is real, I'm going to die*.

As I moved forward to get the slack out of my gunner's restraint, I looked over to the right door for Jerry so we could follow procedure by linking arms and sitting on the floor. He was still sitting there, stunned, on a small wooden box, each hand on a gun grip, staring out the doorway. Then, thankfully, everything went black. After I came around I became aware of a crackling, crunching sound. I thought that it must be the team we had re-supplied. When I was able to twist partially free, what I saw terrified me. The sound of people walking in the bush was actually a fire burning its way to the helicopter. I immediately began struggling to get free, locate my .38 pistol, and take the easy way out before burning to death. To my great relief, our friends in the Kingbee came back to hover over the fire at full power. It worked. They blew out the fire.

After helping me, the pilot said we had to get Jack, the IP, out. Crushed in the cockpit, he was obviously done for, but we had to try. While pulling on the jammed pilot's door, a bright red streak suddenly whooshed between my knees. I thought *what a beautiful sight, the contrast between the red and lush green jungle*. There was another 'whoosh,' and the pilot said, 'The rockets are cooking off, let's get out of here.' After hearing our emergency beeper, a slick came in and dropped a rope to pull us out. As we cleared the tops of the trees, our aircraft exploded with a red fiery mushroom cloud that rose above the trees. The other gunner, Jerry Cooper? After seeing him in the doorway, I never saw him again. A 'Bright Light' team was inserted at the crash site that night, and remained on watch until the fire cooled enough to remove the bodies. We were taken to Duc Lap, and we were then flown by the Kingbee we had narrowly missed to Ban Me Thuot East.

While recovering from wounds in the Can Ranh Bay hospital, the squadron guys visited, wearing various uniforms with no insignia. Some of them kept the nurses busy, while others spray-painted

The original Forward Air Controller (FAC) mount was Cessna's O-1 series "Bird Dog." Green Hornet missions normally were overseen by a FAC carrying a seasoned SOG member, called a "Covey Rider." FAC aircraft, such as this O-1G, carried rockets for marking targets for strike aircraft. (U.S. Air Force)

## Chapter 3: Into the Mouth of the Cat

green hornets on desks and beds. Even my leg cast sported a green hornet."

Although *gun-shy* from the accident, Galvan went back in the air, into combat. He says:

"The crash and the deaths psychologically scarred me. I did my job, but I was frightened all the time of history repeating itself."

After the war, Galvan continued to battle with "survivor's guilt" and self-blame. He persevered, however, and went on to complete an Air Force career.

The move from Tuy Hoa to the larger air facility at Cam Ranh Bay resulted from the cessation of operations following the transfer of the 31st Tactical Fighter Wing. Although the drawdown was gaining momentum, the 20th was needed to support VNAF operations with the 5th Special Forces. Beginning in late November, the 20th's UH-1Ps were gradually replaced by UH-1Ns, which the Air Force selected to upgrade its Huey fleet. The UH-1N was well suited to the Green Hornet mission, having a greater payload capacity and twin engine safety. Initially developed by Bell for the Canadian Armed Forces, the twin Huey was purchased simultaneously by the Air Force and Navy. Deliveries to the Air Force totaled 79 UH-1Ns, with the 20th's fleet completely converted by March 1971. Many of the UH-1Ps were crated for shipment to Hill AFB, Utah.

The N Model was powered by two Pratt & Whitney PT6T-3 turbine engines, having a total output of 1,800 shp. Its maximum gross weight was 10,000 pounds, with a top speed of 142 mph, and the maximum range at mission gross weight was 260 miles. The twin could carry 14 passengers, plus pilot and 220 U.S. gallons of fuel. Like their predecessors, the twins mounted GAU-2B/A and LAU-59/A weapons. In lieu of the miniguns, the Ns often carried XM-94 rapid-fire 40mm hand-operated grenade launchers. The XM-94 had an 800-round capacity, an effective range of nearly 5,000 feet, and could fire 400 rounds per minute. Often a minigun was mounted on one side, with the XM-94 in the opposite door.

### Drawdown

Although most cross-border missions had ceased during mid-1970, the Green Hornets continued supporting the VNAF, occasionally making emergency pickups. This support followed the South Vietnamese Army during *Lam Son 719*, which was the invasion of Laos during early 1971 to deny the enemy supply routes. Although American ground troops were not allowed to cross the border, President Nixon authorized unlimited air support for the invasion force. When SOG shifted its CCS operation to the Task Force I Advisory Element at Da Nang in 1971, the 20th SOS followed, flying troop carrier missions with large groups of aircraft. Having become accustomed to working in small groups, Green Hornet crews gained valuable experience in large scale troop movements. Providing eight Hueys throughout September for daily support of the task force at Marble Mountain proved even more demanding. On almost every sortie, the Hueys were fired upon. The squadron also operated periodically out of sub-FOL Quan Loi in support of Kingbees, plus two aircraft and crews were assigned for more than two months to the Special Forces training facility at Long Thanh, near Saigon. The assignment had Green Hornet crews making several extractions of indigenous soldiers training to be recon team leaders.

On 1 September the 14th Special Operations Wing was deactivated, and the 20th was assigned to the 483rd Tactical Airlift Wing. The squadron still had available between 15 and 18 UN-1Ns, half of which were armed with the XM-74. The single loss of a Green Hornet Huey in 1971 occurred on 18 October due to tail rotor failure. The two pilots managed to escape the aircraft after it crashed into the South China Sea a half-mile off shore.

A former Green Hornet told of a chilling mission that also occurred in October 1971. An Army sergeant had walked out of the jungle into the fire base at Loc Ninh, South Vietnam. Having escaped his captors in Cambodia, the soldier gave information affirming that U.S. soldiers were being held prisoner in North Vietnamese strongholds in Cambodia. A night mission was launched on which three Special Forces soldiers made a HALO (High Altitude-Low Opening) parachute jump near Krek, Cambodia, to locate fellow POWs the escapee had mentioned. Tragically the trio was captured, blinded during torture, and slipped a radio to call for help. The trap was set.

An orbiting "King" C-130 command post picked up the POWs' message and relayed it to an operations center. Cobra gunships from the Army's 334th Assault Helicopter Company were sent, along with two VNAF Kingbees to attempt a rescue. The enemy was waiting and sprung the trap, decimating the rescue force. An element of the 20th SOS, staging as backup at the SF camp at Quan Loi, South Vietnam, was then given the go-ahead. Two gunships and a slick were vectored at treetop level to the site by a FAC, while two gunships served as backup. Amid a fierce firefight, the slick was able to rescue the three badly injured commandos with McGuire rigs, and fly them to Saigon for treatment and debriefing. For their courage and determination, the Green Hornet crewmen were awarded Distinguished Flying Crosses.

The more powerful Cessna O-2 replaced the O-1 during the late 1960s. Air Force FAC aircraft were dispersed among five Tactical Air Support Squadrons (TASS), all of which were based in Vietnam, except the 23rd TASS at NKP. FACs usually were attached to field combat units. This O-2A, seen at Phu Cat AB in 1970, wears a Raven zap, representing the covert FACs that operated across the fence. (Roger Besecker)

49

Tragedy continued until year's end when a Huey slick was downed by ground fire near Saigon on 4 December 1971. The crew was returning to Saigon on a non-combat mission, when the pilot spotted what appeared to be a rocket site near a rice paddy. When they went down for a closer look, enemy soldiers raked the aircraft with gunfire. Despite severe wounds, SGT Thomas E. Fike stayed on his M-60 machine gun and killed a number of enemy before he died. The other crew chief, SGT King, was severely wounded. The pilots managed to fly the UH-1N four miles beyond the site and land before the engines seized. The aircraft was recovered and repaired, and placed back on flying status. Its recovery was short lived, as it was again shot down, this time in Cambodia on 3 February 1972.

The Green Hornets were launching from Plei Djerang, South Vietnam, supporting teams across the border in Cambodia. Things were too quiet; there was an eerie lull in enemy activity; kids from the local village did not pay their usual visit. The sense that something was brewing was confirmed when hordes of NVA troops were detected moving down the Trail in Cambodia. President Nixon's drawdown made the enemy bolder, and they were massing for a major attack. Additional teams were sent out, hopefully, to snatch a prisoner who would talk.

Upon landing at Plei Djerang, the Hornet crew was met by a FAC pilot who said, "We're going to put in a five-man team with plans to leave them until they go 'hot' or get a prisoner." Remembering that the FAC also said, "This is going to be a little tough," the pilots, Donald Hickman and Bruce Knapp, agreed to exchange some of their high explosive rockets for "nails," which were rocket heads packing hundreds of small steel darts—strictly anti-personnel for prepping an LZ.

The VNAF slick dropped off the team, which disappeared into the jungle. Immediately after radioing "team okay," the team came under heavy fire, and was pinned down on three sides. Both Green Hornet gunships made repeated passes, firing rockets just yards from the team. The crew of Gun Lead heard the familiar sound of bullets hitting their Huey; holes appeared in the nose bubble. Lights flickered across the master caution panel, and crew chief Robert Hall called, "Boss, got a hole in the transmission—oil coming out of the hole the size of a quarter!" The next call was, "Right gunner's hit!"

After suffering a head wound, Jon McDaniel got back on his minigun and, mad as a hornet, squeezed both triggers, spraying 4,000 rounds per minute. Both generators went dead, knocking out the miniguns. Knapp and Hickman knew it was time to head for safety. After setting down in a field of cut bamboo, the crew came under fire as they made their way to the rope ladders dangling from the hovering slick, which had followed them down. It took two more gunships, Army Cobras, and A-1 Skyraiders to suppress ground fire long enough to rescue the team. The Huey—the last one the Green Hornets would lose to the enemy—was destroyed later that day by VNAF Skyraiders.

Jim Fudge, who was part of the crew of the rescue bird "Green Hornet Two," says:

"We rescued the crew after firing all but 60 rounds of our combined load of over 15,000 rounds, and rockets and grenades."

The crew was flying one of the few special-request missions the squadron carried out during early 1972. One of those missions marked the bitter end of the 20th SOS, when it was ordered to stand down in March 1972.

The Green Hornet/Special Forces partnership worked very well. At the working level the Green Hornets were fiercely loyal to Special Forces; such was not the case up the chain of command. The order to the 20th to stand down came to Hornet operations by telephone. The operations officer on duty was Major Hershel King,

The North American OV-10A "Bronco" proved to be the ultimate FAC aircraft. Heavily armed, and offering superb visibility and twin engine safety, the Bronco replaced O-1 and O-2 models in all five TASS's. (U.S. Air Force)

who made known his opposition to the order. Present was SF SGT Rudy Cooper, who continues:

"The major put up such a stink because there was a team in the field, and a stand-down would strand them out there. The major read the riot act over the phone to whoever was on the other end of the line. I think it was a colonel or brigadier general in Saigon. Major King lost his career over it. We had to find some Army assets to go out and rescue the team."

Green Hornet Paul "JJ" Jensen summarizes his experience with the 20th SOS:

"What made the 20th SOS so special was not just the missions, but the people who carried out the missions. It was an honor to serve with men of this caliber. We all had a job to do, and we did it without reservation. The professionalism with which we executed our duties cannot be compared to anything else in life. After war and service with SOG, everything else became irrelevant. 'Slicks' were my specialty. There was something about the rescue that gave me a warm feeling, knowing that we were their last hope, and would go to any length to get our guys off the ground, and out of the hell we put them into. I felt very responsible for those I inserted, and much relieved when they were extracted. For those who didn't make it, I can only hope that I did my best.

I'll never forget the good times and the humor we found in the least little things: like walking into the latrine at Ban Me Thuot one day to see that someone had inscribed on the wall, 'Dear God, please stop this war.' On my second trip to the 'john' that day, I doubled over with laughter as someone had written below the original inscription, 'Dear G.I., I didn't start it!'"

# 4

## Above and Beyond

The Green Hornets brushed shoulders with danger so often that it was inevitable that a squadron member would be recommended to receive the Medal of Honor.

At 25 years old, Lieutenant James P. Fleming was razzed about being a youngster among the squadron's pilots, who were much older and higher ranking career pilots. It did not help that he flew slicks, which were viewed as airborne taxis by the swaggering gunship pilots. Fleming did his best to take the rivalry in stride; after all, he had been elevated to aircraft commander status after five months of combat flying.

It was only Fleming's second day as an aircraft commander when he would be faced with a life or death decision. Early on 26 November 1968, Fleming and a new copilot, Major Paul E. McClellan, inserted Recon Team *Chisel* into Cambodia's *Target Tango 51*. It appeared that the enemy did not detect the insertion, so the team stealthily made its way toward a wide river to monitor enemy boat traffic.

The Green Hornet flight returned to Duc Co, and in the afternoon slipped another team into Cambodia. Team Chisel, in the meantime, hid in thick underbrush overlooking the river—when they were attacked by a large enemy force. Team leader SSGT Ancil "Sonny" Franks, along with SGT Charles Hughes and Captain Randolph Harrison, and four montagnards, were trapped. Surrounded on three sides, their only escape route was the impassable river. They knew they would be cut down if they tried to swim to safety.

Knowing that they would be a prize for the hard-core North Vietnamese Army soldiers, who were arriving in large numbers, the team members radioed for gunship support and immediate extraction. Thirty miles away, none of the crewmen in the five Hueys enroute to a fueling site heard the team's calls for help. But forward air controller Major Charles E. Anonsen, flying in the area, was able to pick up the weak radio signal and make out the urgent message. Leonard Gonzales, who was one of the Green Hornet gunship pilots, continues:

"The flight of two gunships and three slicks that inserted the Special Forces team was at a refueling site east of Duc Co. I had just gotten airborne when I received a coded message from the FAC that the team we had inserted was on the verge of being overrun. I relayed the message to the three slicks on the ground, and they immediately took off. Since my wing man and I were airborne I pushed the power to the maximum setting the helicopter could handle. Our airspeed never reached 100 knots, because we were fully loaded with fuel and ammo. As we raced toward the trapped team, a slick passed us. I told my copilot not to worry, because they could not do anything without our firepower."

With the Green Hornet flight inbound, Anonsen surveyed the area. He spotted only two clearings nearby that might accommodate a helicopter. One 20 yards away appeared to be too small and grown over, however, the other, 100 yards from the team, was

## Chapter 4: Above and Beyond

Captain James P. Fleming shortly after being awarded the Medal of Honor. (U.S. Air Force)

much larger. But RT Chisel was so tightly pinned down by heavy fire that it was impossible for them to move.

Adding to the seemingly impossible chance of pulling off a rescue, the Green Hornet transport Hueys had only enough fuel for a quick extraction. Anonsen briefed the Huey crews when they arrived, and then had the team mark its position with red smoke grenades. The smoke pinpointed the team, which was returning withering fire, and beating back repeated assaults.

Flying the lead gunship, Major Leonard Gonzales and his copilot, Capt. Perry Russell, unleashed rockets, while their gunners, SSGT William R. Combs and SGT Kevin R. Kogan, poured withering minigun fire on the enemy. According to Gonzales:

"I started a descent away from the team in a deep spiral dive and turned back, coming out on top of the trees. During the dive I spotted the team, and flew right over them as my gunners fired their miniguns around them. Captain Miller's gunship also fired miniguns. I then made a turn 90 degrees to the left, and after two minutes turned right, and made a 180-degree turn to come from the opposite direction. We provided maximum firepower to the Special Forces team to break them out. Normally the firepower of four miniguns enabled us in other rescue missions to break the back of the enemy, so a slick helicopter could land and grab the trapped team. On this mission it was not possible."

Lined up closely behind *Gunship Lead* was the second gunship, flown by Captain David W. Miller and Major Russell J. Simonetta. They too fired rockets as their gunners, SSGTs Ronald W. Brodeur and Dennis C. Miller, poured minigun fire onto the enemy.

Orbiting nearby, Fleming saw the gunships destroy two 12.7mm machine guns only 200 yards from Team Chisel. Despite the onslaught from the air, enemy fire not only persisted, but was now directed at the Hueys.

Although he knew he was in trouble after machine gun fire riddled his gunship, Miller made two more passes in trail with Gonzales. A second volley of machine gun fire killed the engine of Miller's Huey. He radioed that they were going down and auto-rotated into a clearing. When Major Dale L. Eppinger, pilot of *Flight Lead*, heard Miller say he was going down, he and his copilot, Major Gene A. Hamman, followed Miller down, landed immediately behind him, and lifted off with the downed crew. Within minutes, the enemy arrived and destroyed Miller's Huey. Critically low on fuel, Eppinger headed for Duc Co.

Gonzales and his crew continued their firing runs around the trapped team. One of the slicks went below fuel minimums and had to leave. The situation was critical. Anonsen worried not only that the rescue force was now down to two helicopters, but that both had little fuel and ammunition left. Fleming maintained his orbit waiting for Anonsen to give the go-ahead to go in. The enemy was relentless. It was time to attempt the rescue.

On Anonsen's cue, the team tried to move to the small clearing near the river, while Fleming received word to move in for the pick-up. Hoping that the riverbanks would shield them, Fleming made a high-speed approach, skimming the water, running a gauntlet of enemy fire, while his gunners and copilot returned fire as they searched for the team. When he discovered that his Huey would not fit into the small clearing, Fleming, in a masterful display of flying skill, nosed his Huey into the riverbank, with its tail boom extended over the water. Gonzales continues:

"I positioned my gunship about 50 feet above the slick, and both miniguns opened fire. Both my gunship and Fleming's slick were driven off when the enemy opened fire and rushed the team."

When the NVA attacked, a team member radioed, "They've got us! They've got us! Get out! Get out!" Fleming backed away from the bank and climbed out, while gunners Cook and Johnson put their M60 machine guns to work. As soon as Fleming broke clear, Gonzales rolled in and fired one of his remaining rockets, and then made three minigun passes. When Fleming heard a *claymore* mine detonate, and saw an enemy soldier's body hurled into the air, he radioed, "What's going on down there?" "We blew them back," a team member answered, "but we're almost out of claymores and can't hold out much longer."

It appeared that Recon Team Chisel was doomed. Fleming radioed Anonsen, "We'll give it one more try." Nearly out of fuel and ammunition, Gonzales added, "I'll make one more pass over 'em, but then I've got to get out of here." Knowing that it was now or never, Fleming and his crew bravely headed back into the lion's den. During the descent, Anonsen told the team to prepare to detonate its remaining claymores and get onto the riverbank at all costs. Ringing their position with claymores, the team knew its predicament; they also knew that Fleming's chance of getting in and surviving another run through the lethal gauntlet was remote.

Fleming again dropped down, skittered across the brown water, and nosed into the riverbank. This time the team was there, and so were the NVA soldiers, fully aware that their fat target would hover in the same place. A fierce battle broke out as the team detonated their claymores and ran for the chopper. As Gonzales again provided minigun fire from directly overhead, Fleming's gunners also covered the team's dash for freedom.

Despite the heavy volume of fire and team members clambering aboard, Fleming held his Huey in a rock-steady hover. Bullets shattered the Huey's windshield, snapping past the pilots' heads; yet Fleming, unflinching, held the chopper snug against the river bank. While Fleming's gunner, Johnson, worked frantically to clear his jammed M60, Cook, on the opposite M60, fired with one hand, while pulling men aboard with the other as they reached for the dangling rope ladder. Fleming spotted NVA soldiers along the riverbank, and the team killed three who had worked their way within a few yards of the helicopter.

Although Captain Harrison had not appeared, Fleming knew he had to get out of there before the massive volume of fire knocked his Huey down into the river. As he gripped the controls to pull away from the bank, Harrison broke through the brush, firing behind him. He jumped into the water, grabbed the rope ladder, and

## Chapter 4: Above and Beyond

Fred Cook grabbed his hand. In a hail of bullets, Fleming lifted away, dragging the rope ladder in the river.

As Fleming climbed out of the area, Gonzales fired his last rocket, and his gunners fired their remaining minigun rounds.

Fleming and his copilot, McClellan, had been so focused that they didn't notice their bullet-shattered windshield until they felt air rushing in. The fuel gauge read empty when they landed at Duc Co. Fleming later commented:

"The first time we went in I wasn't really conscious of the danger. You know, it was what we had trained to do. And so we did it. But then it all got to me. Dave Miller getting shot down, the heaviest hostile fire I'd seen...frankly, I was scared to death!"

Although the odds were in favor of the enemy, Fleming refused to allow "his" team to be killed or captured. He overcame his fear, and mustered the courage necessary to save the seven men of Recon Team Chisel. One expression of gratitude not printed in Fleming's official citation came from team member Randy Harrison who, in true recon spirit, after the mission grabbed Fleming's head, stuck his tongue in the startled pilot's ear, and exclaimed, "You sweet motherfucker!"

A short time later, Fleming again became irked when fellow pilots razzed him, this time about leaving the Green Hornets. But they weren't kidding. Young Jim Fleming had orders to travel to Washington, D.C., where the President would hang a pale blue ribbon around his neck. Besides Fleming's Medal of Honor, Gonzales was recommended for the Air Force Cross, becoming the first Hispanic to receive the award.

# 5

# Between the Wars

Since the 20th's deactivation during the war, only the 317th SOS at Hurlburt Field operated UH-1F, -P, and -N variants for special operations, until it too closed its doors in 1974. In 1975 Air Force leaders, intent on maintaining a foothold in joint services unconventional warfare doctrine, decided that a small helicopter force was necessary to enhance their special operations capabilities. Therefore, the 20th SOS was reactivated at Hurlburt Field, Florida, on 1 January 1976, to become the third special operations squadron under the Tactical Air Command's 1st Special Operations Wing. Although the primary mission of the 20th SOS was to conduct unconventional warfare, it would also be capable of performing humanitarian, civic action, and rescue operations.

Since the UH-1 and H-3 series helicopters already existed in the Air Force inventory, it was decided that they would equip the newly formed unit. At reactivation, the squadron had only one UH-1N (s/n 69-6654), and nearly one year would pass before the squadron reached its authorized strength of six UH-1Ns and four CH-3Es. With its full complement of helicopters, flying operations focused on training and support of the 1st Special Operations Wing's Combat Control Team (CCT). The CCT comprised pathfinder commandos who were air traffic controllers.

The following are the recollections of Col. Michael Collins, who was assigned to the Green Hornets from 1976 to 1979:

"I came into the 20th from flight school, and was one of five lieutenants assigned. Most of the squadron's first crewmembers consisted of battle-hardened pilots, flight engineers, and gunners from Vietnam. It was a humbling feeling for a 2nd Lieutenant right out of flight school to be placed with such a dynamic mix of characters with combat experience.

At first the squadron had a full complement of UH-1N gunships, but had only one CH-3E for the 'tuna boat' pilots. Flying time was a premium at first, and it took almost a year to accumulate four CH-3Es for 16 CH-3E pilots. As a lieutenant, my flying time was limited. We ended up going to Luke AFB, Arizona, where our sister reserve CH-3E squadron was gracious enough to provide additional flying time.

The first 20th SOS change of command during the post-Vietnam war period involved the traditional signing of a tail rotor blade. Lt. Col. Robert E. Mayo (left) turned over the squadron to Lt. Col. John Roberts in late 1978. Holding the blade for Roberts to sign is 20th CH-3E pilot Lt. Michael Collins. (U.S. Air Force)

## Chapter 5: Between the Wars

This photo, taken at the West German-Czechoslovakian border in 1984 by a U.S. Army AH-1 Cobra crewman, dramatically illustrates the importance of the J-CATCH program. The face-off between the Cobra and the Mi-24 HIND ended with the HIND suffering a mishap and crashing. (Larry Remer)

The squadron accomplished several significant events and projects between 1976 and 1979. We were the first Air Force squadron, among both fixed- and rotary-wing, to train and fly with night vision goggles. Captain Joe Vallimont was sent to Fort Rucker to receive training from the Army, and returned to give classes and flight instruction to both UH-1N and CH-3E crews.

In 1978 the 20th participated in its first cold weather exercise, which took place at Griffis AFB, New York. The area was experiencing one of its coldest winters. Our mission was to transport Army Special Forces troops to various LZs, where the majority of our crewmembers experienced their first *whiteouts*.

From the 20th, I gained friendship and respect for the experienced crewmembers. As a young lieutenant in the squadron I received the usual harassment, but my mentors from those days guided me through a successful Air Force career. Gary Wiekle, now a retired colonel, is one of those who helped me, and did a superb job reactivating the squadron. Several years later he became one of the squadron's commanders. Wiekle can be credited as one of the individuals who made the 20th the premier helicopter squadron in the Air Force. It remains so to this day.

One of my mentors and a close friend, Jim Woolworth, helped build the CH-3E section into a first-class operation. He was one of the best helicopter pilots I had ever flown with. He taught me the real way to fly helicopters, and I credit my success of 4,000 accident-free flying hours to his tutelage.

The 20th crewmembers were the cream of the crop, all being highly dedicated and experienced. Those who served during the early stages of the unit's reactivation laid the foundation for the modern Green Hornets. That tradition still stands, and only the best helicopter pilots are found in the 20th. I was very proud to serve with that first group, and I owe all of them a huge thanks for teaching me the ropes."

One of four of the 20th SOS UH-1Ns modified for the J-CATCH program. The gun camera system beneath the aircraft was normally kept in a stowed position, since it had to extend well beyond the skids to be effective. This Huey's gray and green camouflage deviated significantly from the leopard scheme applied to J-CATCH aggressor aircraft. (U.S. Air Force)

*Green Hornets: The History of the U.S. Air Force 20th Special Operations Squadron*

Two CH-3Es participated in the J-CATCH program in which 20th SOS helicopters played the role of aggressor aircraft to test helicopter-versus-helicopter combat tactics. Like 20th Hueys painted the special scheme, the pair of CH-3Es wore two distinct leopard patterns, that seen here on s/n 69-5811 showing less gray background. (Bill Curry)

**J-CATCH**

Throughout the late 1970s Green Hornet crewmen and their aircraft performed a wide variety of missions, including search and rescue, tactical training exercises, and testing new equipment. A monumental task performed by the 20th during that period was *J-CATCH*, for *Joint Countering Attack Helicopters*. Having studied the development and increasing number of armed helicopters in potentially adversarial nations—where tacticians were certain to have studied successful U.S. helicopter operations—Air Force leaders saw the importance of developing tactics to counter the threat. They also felt that a test program would provide valuable information about the helicopter's ability to stand up against other aircraft types, including high-performance fixed-wing varieties.

Credit for the J-CATCH concept goes to the U.S. Army, whose leaders two decades earlier expressed concern that medevac helicopters were easy prey. The first tests were conducted under *Project MASSTER* (Mobile Army Sensor Systems Test, Evaluation and Review), which was established at Fort Hood, Texas, in 1969. In 1971 the Army's Combat Development Evaluation Center pitted AH-1G Cobra gunships against Navy F-4 Phantoms. Later, Air Force rescue helicopters served as targets in training exercises.

Since the helicopter was expected to do nothing more than attempt to evade an aggressor aircraft, the Army began exploring helicopter-versus-helicopter tactics. The program, called Air Combat Engagement (ACE), proved the need for enhancing the helicopter's air-to-air capability. Early tests had proven that, in certain situations, helicopters could destroy other aircraft; however, specific details were not documented.

The ACE program, along with input from Air Force Air Rescue leaders, was incorporated into the J-CATCH program, which got its official start at NASA's Langley facility in May 1978. Both fixed- and rotary-wing pilots from the Army, Marines, and Air Force participated in the first phase, which examined armed and unarmed helicopters against fighter aircraft. Since the 20th special-

This CH-3E, nicknamed "Spot," wears what is believed to be the later leopard paint scheme. The rare aircraft is seen displayed at NAS Pensacola shortly after it was transferred from the 20th to a rescue squadron. (Jim Burns)

## Chapter 5: Between the Wars

ized in unconventional warfare, and its crews were skilled in precision low-level navigation, it was the natural choice to assume the role of the aggressor *Red Force*.

Beginning in January 1978, 20th SOS personnel worked with various Tactical Air Command officers to make the transformation to a threat helicopter force. While 20th helicopters underwent modification for J-CATCH, aircrews pored over intelligence information to learn their opponent's tactics. The top secret J-CATCH reportedly included a Soviet helicopter instructor pilot on the training staff.

The helicopters (two CH-3Es and four UH-1Ns) were equipped by Emerson Electric with video camera systems that simulated weapon systems of Soviet helicopters. Corresponding electronic equipment installed in the aircraft recorded the effectiveness of simulated gun, rocket, and missile systems. Camera-assisted Mini-TAT chain guns, which were loaned by the Canadian government, were mounted to the underside of the CH-3E aircraft. To complete the transformation to Soviet-built lookalikes, J-CATCH aggressor helicopters were painted in "Leopard" camouflage schemes of light green, dark green, and brown blotches over gray. So popular was the leopard scheme that it was used by the Green Hornets until the mid-1980s.

The six Red Force aircraft were first pitted against a *Blue Force* anti-armor team, consisting of three Army AH-1S Cobras and two OH-58A Scout helicopters at Fort Rucker, Alabama. The two-year program was divided into six phases, and it was not until Phase Three that the *Red Force* engaged F-4, A-7, F-15, and A-10 aircraft. Each aircraft type flew against the Red Force for one week, first dealing with a non-threatening helicopter, and working up to opposing the entire Red Force. Faced with the skill and tenacity of Green Hornet aircrews, fighter pilots learned quickly that the armed helicopter threat could no longer be taken lightly. Former Green Hornet Robert Hall adds:

"We flew against the best the Air Force and Army had, and when we won, we would brief the opposing pilots, much to their dismay."

In contrast, veteran Army pilots maintain that the results are inconclusive, since the Air Force flew against training units, not line units.

While 20th SOS aircraft flew as aggressors against U.S. Army helicopters, they simultaneously conducted joint operations to achieve common goals. For example, in June 1978 CH-3Es of the

Serial number 69-6654 in 1980. Although four Green Hornet Hueys participated in the J-CATCH program, it's possible that at least two additional UH-1Ns were painted the special scheme. Modelers may be interested to know that the official colors were Brown (30118), Dark Green (34092), and Light Green (34102) over the base color Gray (36231). (Phillip Huston)

20th flew as pathfinders for a flight of 22 Army helicopters from Fort Benning, Georgia. Dubbed *Operation Night Hawk*, the mission not only marked the first time such a joint operation took place, it foreshadowed the 20th's skillful role as pathfinders for an attack helicopter force.

Besides J-CATCH, the squadron stayed busy throughout 1979 testing new equipment, including a long-range navigation system, and honing its special operations skills. In September Air Force officials gave the go-ahead to consider replacement of the UH-1Ns. When the U.S. embassy in Tehran was overrun on 4 November 1979, the 20th's parent unit, the 1st SOW, immediately began training for an attempt to rescue the hostages. Helicopters were to be included; however, those flown by the 20th SOS did not meet the demands of the mission. Although Green Hornet pilots did fit the mission, they were only briefly considered for training to fly the Navy's large RH-53 helicopters selected for the ill-fated mission. It was later determined that the Marine pilots who flew the RH-53s lacked experience in specific technical aspects of the mission, such as the use of night vision goggles, and flying in desert conditions. It was the failure of the hostage rescue attempt that prompted the Vice Chief of Staff of the Air Force on 14 May 1980 to order the re-assignment of nine Sikorsky HH-53 helicopters, complete with aircrew and maintenance personnel, from Air Rescue to the 1st SOW. Although the faster, larger helicopter would provide special operations with long-range, heavy lift capabilities, the sudden displacement of such a large package did not set well with the Air Rescue community.

**PAVE LOW**

A YCH-53A prototype first flew in October 1964, with the Marines taking delivery of the first production models. Two months prior to the Marine CH-53's introduction to the Vietnam war in January 1967, the Air Force had borrowed a pair of CH-53As for evaluation. The two were assigned to the 48th Air Rescue and Recovery Squadron (ARRS) at Eglin AFB. Meanwhile, four HH-3E pilots and three crew chiefs of Detachment 5, 38th ARRS, underwent CH-53A training at Sikorsky. Pleased with the aircraft, Air Force leaders adopted a rescue version of the CH-53A—designated HH-53B—to augment the HH-3E and beef up rescue capabilities. Eight HH-53Bs were built, with the first deployment to the war zone occurring in fall 1967. Two became combat losses, one of which was shot down by a MiG-21. Two were later assigned to the 1550th Aircrew Training and Test Wing (ATTW) at Kirtland AFB, New Mexico, for the development of a *Limited Night Recovery*

Armed with miniguns and rockets, a Green Hornet UH-1N flies over a stateside range. The leopard scheme was used until 1985. (U.S. Air Force)

## Chapter 5: Between the Wars

*System* (LNRS). This system was the beginning of a series of H-53 upgrades that would provide combat rescue forces with an all-weather, nighttime, low-level capability.

Charles Isackson, who worked with the test aircraft as a HH-53 crew chief, remembers:

"LNRS was the modification used for low-light-level rescue missions in Southeast Asia. It was the predecessor of the PAVE LOW aircraft that the Air Force designated the MH-53. The two LNRS HH-53Bs were serial numbers 66-14428 and -14429. These aircraft were distinguished by a shielded black box protruding from the lower fuselage just left of the nose gear. Radar Homing and Warning (RHAW) probes were just above and outboard of the nose access door. Pilots who served in the Vietnam conflict stated that the only useful purpose of the RHAW was to give you just enough time to kiss your ass goodbye. All of the unit's HH-53s were configured with inflight refueling probes, and two 650-gallon drop tanks. A special stop had to be incorporated on the right door gunner's minigun mount to prevent him from shooting off the tip of the large tank."

Green Hornet Huey helicopters assigned to Operation BAT wore large signs making known their role in supporting law enforcement agencies targeting drug trafficking. The UH-1N s/n 69-6653 is seen here at Bimini, Bahamas, during the mid-1980s. (Chris Lenahan)

Five of the surviving six HH-53Bs eventually equipped the 551st SOS at Kirtland AFB. One went to the 1550th ATTW, where it was destroyed in a crash in September 1981. The 1550th ATTW, which had been activated in April 1971 at Hill AFB, Utah, was transferred to Kirtland in February 1976, and in May 1984 became the 1550th Combat Crew Training Wing (CCTW).

Evaluation of the LNRS evolved into an electronics modification program codenamed PAVE LOW. Outfitted with advanced radar systems, an HH-53B (s/n 66-14433) served as the prototype HH-53H Pave Low II. The HH-53H featured a highly sophisticated electronics suite, and a central computer to allow remarkably accurate navigational flying. The aircraft could operate in total darkness and, when conditions permitted, night vision goggles reduced the crew workload. Terrain-following/Terrain-avoidance radar and Forward Looking Infrared Radar (FLIR), along with a projected map display, enabled the crew to follow terrain contours and avoid obstacles, making low-level penetration possible. A symbol generator system, inertial measuring unit, radar warning receiver, and flare/chaff dispensers were also added. Completing the upgrade were an improved secure communications system, a Global Positioning System (GPS), a heads-up display, and specialized gear for various methods of infiltrating and extracting special operations troops.

Following successful tests, nine HH-53Cs were converted to Pave Low IIIs, and transferred from the 1550th ATTW to the 20th SOS in June 1980. In 1986 their designation was changed from HH-53H to MH-53H. Although the "H" prefix stood for "Rescue," and the "M" prefix officially stood for "Multi-mission," the latter came to identify special operations aircraft. The H-53's heavy lifting ability was offset by its size, and powerful rotor downwash.

In September 1980 the 20th SOS transferred its CH-3Es to other units, and plans were made to replace the UH-1Ns with Sikorsky H-60s, although that action was delayed.

When fire ravaged the MGM Hotel in Las Vegas, Nevada, on 21 November 1980, nine helicopters from nearby Nellis AFB quickly came to the rescue. Included were three 20th SOS Hueys, and this CH-3E, one of three from the 302nd SOS, whose aircraft were manned by both 20th and 302nd crews. (Las Vegas Sun)

61

*Green Hornets: The History of the U.S. Air Force 20th Special Operations Squadron*

Three of the four Huey crewmen posing with bales of drugs confiscated in OPBAT were 40th ARRS personnel temporarily assigned to the 20th SOS. Flight Engineer Chris Lenahan is at left. (Chris Lenahan Collection)

Before the Marine Corps even took their new CH-53As to Vietnam, the Air Force borrowed two for evaluation in late 1966. Pleased with the results, the first Air Force examples were pressed into the rescue service. This former Marine CH-53A was allocated USAF serial number 66-14470. (Tom Maloney)

*Chapter 5: Between the Wars*

The predecessor of PAVE LOW. This was the first of eight CH-53As converted to HH-53Bs for rescue work. It, and s/n 66-14429, were equipped with a Limited Night Recovery System, which aided rescue in Southeast Asia. Both aircraft were assigned to the 1550th Aircrew Training and Test Wing. All of the unit's HH-53s featured a pair of 650-gallon external fuel tanks and refueling probes. (Charles Isackson)

The Pave Lows and their crews were quickly added to the mix of special aircraft gathered to train for a second attempt to rescue the hostages in Iran. After five months of training for the daunting task, named *Project Honey Badger*, the rescue force remained on standby, since the risk involved was deemed unacceptable. The hostages were released in January 1981, and *Honey Badger* was dissolved.

**Fire at the MGM**

True to its secondary mission involving rescue work, the 20th SOS added to its history pages its work at the second deadliest hotel fire in U.S. history. On the morning of 21 November 1980, fire broke out at the 26-story MGM Hotel in Las Vegas, Nevada. Luckily, at nearby Nellis AFB, Huey crews of the 20th SOS were participating in exercise *Red Flag*, when the deployment commander, Lt. Col. Wayne Corder, received an urgent message: "The MGM Grand is burning—helicopters are needed to rescue the people trapped in the building."

Three Green Hornet UH-1Ns were quickly readied, and joined six other helicopters from Tactical Air Command units temporarily based at Nellis. They were three CH-3Es from the 302nd SOS, and UH-1Ns from the 57th Fighter Weapons Wing, Detachment 1. Some 20th SOS crewmen, including squadron commander Lt. Col. William Takacs, joined CH-3E crews.

Throughout the day, 20th SOS crews flew a total of 13 hours carrying firefighters, paramedics, and supplies to the roof of the burning hotel. They also brought down 36 survivors, and are cred-

To maintain a state of readiness for worldwide deployment, the Green Hornets have long practiced for such events. Here, MH-53s are torn down for shipment aboard C-5 transport aircraft during the 1980s. (U.S. Air Force)

*Green Hornets: The History of the U.S. Air Force 20th Special Operations Squadron*

Having evolved from the line of Air Force H-53s, the MH-53 became the ultimate special operations helicopter. Here, a special operations soldier climbs aboard serial number 68-10356, which accomplished a number of firsts during Operation Desert Storm. (Sean Borland)

## Chapter 5: Between the Wars

ited with saving the lives of five critically injured people. Later they shared with Detachment 1 the grim task of bringing the dead down from the roof. The tragedy claimed 85 lives and injured 700.

**Operation BAT**
There seemed to be no shortage of work for the Green Hornets, and no limitations on the variety of work for which they were selected. Proving once again their adaptability, the unit in May 1983 became part of Vice President Bush's task force on drugs.

For years the Bahamas, Antilles, and Turks and Caicos (BAT) islands in the Caribbean were major connection points in drug smuggling from South America to Florida's southern and eastern seaboards. Federal authorities have determined that 70 percent of the drugs entering the U.S. come through the Bahamas. In June 1982 *Operation BAT*, or *OPBAT*, began as a multi-agency, international operation based in Nassau, Bahamas. Following Congressional legislation in 1981 allowing military assistance to law enforcement, Operation BAT became a cooperative effort between the U.S. Drug Enforcement Agency (DEA) and the Government of the Commonwealth of the Bahamas.

Originally, two Nassau-based DEA helicopters flew daily missions, and were replaced in June 1983 by two UH-1Ns and eight crewmembers of the 20th SOS. On missions, Green Hornet Hueys carried a standard four-man crew, plus four members of the Royal Bahamian Police Strike Team, and a DEA agent. Strike teams were well armed; however, aircrew were not armed, thereby absolving the U.S. government of conducting armed military operations in the Bahamas. U.S. Customs tracked suspect aircraft and gave chase. After being given a fix on the aircraft, Green Hornets launched from Nassau to make the intercept with the strike team. Since smugglers preferred dusk, missions were often flown at night, and with the aid of night vision goggles.

According to Chris Lenahan, who participated as an Air Force crewman:

"The UH-1Ns of the 20th were specially equipped for these missions. Besides the big 'POLICE' signs on the cabin doors, they had a high frequency radio system installed, with a hard antenna mounted along the lower right side of the tail boom. And an Omega navigation system was installed. The Omega system was not GPS-based back then, but used ground stations to get a fix. It did not work well at sunrise and sunset. With this nav system we were permitted to operate VFR at night in the Bahamas. This caused quite a problem for the controllers in the tower at Nassau Airport, as we would get special VFR clearance, and a pilot waiting on the ground heard this on the radio and requested the same clearance. He was usually told to taxi back to the ramp so they could discuss it with him."

Green Hornet crews worked long hours, often over water. Shortly after setting up shop at Nassau, on 4 July 1983, Operation BAT netted a Cessna 404 aircraft, its pilot, and nearly 900 pounds of cocaine, plus a 70-foot vessel, and more than 30 tons of marijuana. The 20th workload became so heavy, and their special operations training suffered to the extent that it became necessary to train ARRS crews to perform the OPBAT mission. The 40th ARRS began sending crews to Hurlburt for training, and then to the Bahamas to relieve 20th crews.

On 9 January 1984, UH-1N s/n 69-6644 was lost ten miles north of Nassau due to a failure of its fuel system. The Huey crashed into the ocean, killing the pilot, Captain Dyke H. Whitbeck; copilot Lieutenant Thomas L. Hamby; and the flight engineer, SSGT Edgardo L. Acha. Also lost were the DEA agent, and one of the Bahamian police officers aboard. The gunner, SSGT Paul B. Cartter, was seriously injured.

The Green Hornets mourned their losses and carried on the mission. In September a chase of a DC-6 cargo aircraft resulted in its capture, along with the crew, and nearly seven tons of marijuana. In December a UH-1N teamed with a U.S. Customs aircraft to chase a drug smuggling aircraft to Sebring, Florida, where the smugglers and the aircraft, plus its load of drugs, were seized.

The longest lasting mission spanned four weeks during November and December 1984. Crews of the 20th SOS and the 40th ARRS stood 24-hour alert blocking air routes through the Bahamas, while ships blockaded the Columbian coast, and ground troops moved against the country's marijuana harvest. The massive undertaking was dubbed *Operation Wagon Wheel*, whose air elements were called *Operation Hat Trick*. The multi-agency mission was the largest anti-drug operation in the history of the U.S. drug war.

On 1 October 1985, after having flown more than 3,000 sorties—which led to the capture or destruction of more than $1.5 billion in drugs, plus the smuggler aircraft and vessels, and many of their crew—the 20th turned over its UH-1Ns and the OPBAT mission to the 48th ARRS at Homestead AFB, Florida.

**PAVE LOW Happenings**
While Green Hornet Huey crews chased drug smugglers, the nine-aircraft Pave Low section was kept equally busy, mainly with training and worldwide deployment exercises. Although such operations did not involve combat, they were high risk, as evidenced by the loss of two HH-53Hs in crashes during late 1984. One of the crashes occurred in the Philippines, claiming the lives of all six crewmen.

On 22 May 1984 an Army-Air Force agreement was signed transferring short-range special operations forces support to the Army. Some officials preferred that the entire package be signed over to the Army. The Army had no long-range helicopters capable of such support, and only a few HH-53 Pave Lows were available. The Army didn't want them, but the Air Force did, which kept alive the HH-53 update program to equip the newly combined Air Force rescue and special operations force.

After extensive modifications, the MH-53H became the MH-53J, or Pave Low III Enhanced, the first four of which were rolled out on 17 July 1987. The 20th SOS began flying the MH-53J in 1988. Eventually all 41 H-53s in the Air Force inventory were converted to MH-53Js. The MH-53J wears armor plating, and armament consisting of any combination of the time-tested 7.62mm miniguns or .50 cal. machine guns. Its crew consists of two pilots, two flight engineers, and two gunners. The Pave Low's mission became low-level, long-range, undetected penetration into denied areas, day or night, in any weather, for infiltration, extraction, and re-supply of special operations forces. The 20th was authorized 22 MH-53Js, making it the largest squadron in the Air Force Special Operations Command.

Training, which tested the limits of Pave Low aircraft and crews, included flying in mountainous terrain at Dobbins AFB, Georgia, and Kirtland AFB, New Mexico; shipboard operations aboard various U.S. Navy vessels; and working with special operations troops. The emphasis on training regularly, and in every conceivable aspect of their mission, kept the 20th SOS in a high state of readiness and proficiency. Training in tactics, weapons, flight procedures, and teardown and reassembly of the aircraft under various conditions were commonplace. Skill levels were unmatched, as training became the hallmark of the Green Hornets.

Near the end of 1989, the 20th SOS had just completed a major training exercise when they received word that they would soon face combat in Panama.

**Just Cause**

The Green Hornets endured a non-stop, 1,500-mile deployment in severe weather to be among the first U.S. military forces brought to bear for the invasion of Panama. On 20 December during the first hour of the invasion, which was called *Operation Just Cause*, MH-53J crews of the 20th SOS inserted commandos, and provided fire support and evacuation of the wounded. Combat operations included a three-aircraft assault into Downtown Panama City, a night assault on General Noriega's beach house, and an eight-aircraft assault to take the prison camp at Playa de Golfa. In addition, Green Hornet MH-53Js rescued a Ranger team pinned down by hostile fire, and on 29 December rescued 19 students at El Porvenir. Some Pave Lows sustained battle damage during the 142 combat sorties flown by the squadron.

Operation Just Cause would prove to be a primer for forthcoming battles, when America drew a line in the sand.

# 6

# Sandstorms

Just five days after Iraq invaded Kuwait on 2 August 1990, *Operation Desert Shield* began. America's response included, among aircraft from the U.S. Air Force Special Operations Command, eight Green Hornet MH-53Js, which deployed to Saudi Arabia. In preparation for desert operations, the 20th SOS had logged more than 2,800 zero-visibility landings in dust-out conditions. Prior to Desert Shield evolving into *Operation Desert Storm*, two additional MH-53Js had been sent to Turkey.

In the early morning hours of 17 January 1991, just hours after the President ordered Desert Storm, the 20th SOS launched their MH-53Js from a forward operating site in Saudi Arabia. It fell upon four Pave Lows to sneak across the Iraqi border and punch a hole in the seemingly impenetrable early-warning screen of Hussein's air defenses. As part of *Task Force Normandy*, two Pave Low sections of two aircraft each would lead a flight of eight Army Apache gunships. The Apache crews were to simultaneously destroy two radar stations, thereby opening a corridor for coalition aircraft to begin the air campaign against Hussein's forces.

Flying at 50 feet above the desert, in total darkness, relying completely on computers and sensors, the Pave Low crews used sophisticated equipment to blind enemy radar and surface-to-air missile sites. Before the enemy could react, the Apaches destroyed the two radar stations with laser-guided Hellfire missiles, striking the first blow in the air campaign of the Persian Gulf war.

Within one week of the beginning of the campaign, on 21 January, the 20th SOS would again make their mark in history by performing the first combat rescue behind enemy lines since the Vietnam war.

On that date Navy Lieutenants Devon Jones and Lawrence Slade bailed out of their F-14 when it was hit by an Iraqi missile 160 miles inside Iraq. Green Hornet pilots Captain Thomas Trask and Major Michael Homan and crew (call sign "Moccasin 05") took off in an MH-53J in dense fog after refueling at Arar Airfield, Saudi Arabia, to join the search effort. While they refueled, a pair of A-10A "Sandies" had established radio contact with the F-14 pilot. At the Iraqi border the MH-53 dropped to an altitude of 15 feet. Although warned by the AWACS "Yukon" that missile radar was tracking the Pave Low, the crew flew two search sorties. Nearly six hours after the crash, the Green Hornet crew made radio contact with Lt. Jones. Unbeknownst to the rescue force, Slade had been

Freshly painted in desert camouflage for Operation Desert Storm, this 20th SOS MH-53 wears only a faint U.S. national insignia. (Sean Borland)

*Green Hornets: The History of the U.S. Air Force 20th Special Operations Squadron*

captured. After the Sandies destroyed an enemy truck closing in on Jones, Captain Trask landed the MH-53J to pick up the exhausted but grateful Navy flier.

On 27 February five Pave Lows, along with MH-60G Pave Hawk gunship escorts of the 55th SOS, departed King Fahd Airport, and thundered into Kuwait to regain the U.S. embassy. Special Forces troops aboard the Pave Lows rappelled onto the embassy roof to secure the complex. That same day, when Iraqi troops positioned more than two dozen Scud missile launchers near the border to draw Israel into the war, commandos inserted weeks earlier by Pave Lows laser-painted the launchers for A-10s, which destroyed them all.

Green Hornet Pave Lows were included in the strategic planning for the first wave of the ground war in February. Three MH-53Js were tasked with infiltrating four SEAL teams, whose mission was to report information concerning the movement of enemy ground troops and armor, which was vital to the invading 7th Corps.

Getting the SEAL teams to their reconnaissance sites seemed an insurmountable task, since the Pave Lows had to fly not only through countless missile and anti-aircraft gun sites, but through low visibility caused by smoke, rain, and dust-out conditions.

Although many mission details concerning the Green Hornets in Iraq remain classified, it is known that in 1991 a 20th SOS MH-53J participated in the first U.S./British combat search and rescue effort 200 miles inside Iraq. The 20th SOS was among the Special Operations Forces that remained in the Persian Gulf until early 1993, providing support for *Operations Provide Comfort* and *Southern Watch*.

Familiar with sandstorms, the 20th in October 2001 began supporting *Operation Enduring Freedom* in Afghanistan. The following month, on a mission the details of which remain classified, a Green Hornet Pave Low went down in mountainous Afghanistan in bad weather. The Pave Low was one of two enroute to rescue a special operations member. After several hours of trying to penetrate the poor weather, and with malfunctioning radar, the crew of the other Pave Low located its downed sister ship. Due to the high altitude and extra weight of the downed crew, the Pave Low was barely able to climb from the site. With the engines straining at maximum power, and after several partial aerial refuelings, the Pave Low made it to a secure site to offload injured crewmen. Another Pave Low was lost in Afghanistan on 23 November 2003, taking the lives of three crewmembers.

Another operation that kept the 20th SOS busy during the mid-1990s was *Operation Restore Democracy* in Haiti. In early 1994 the 20th SOS took over from the 21st SOS support of *Operation Provide Promise*, the humanitarian relief effort in the Balkans. The Pave Lows and crews stood alert at Brindisi Air Base, Italy, for combat search and rescue for NATO aircraft involved in *Operations Deny Flight* and *Provide Promise*. The 21st SOS, which also

Three Green Hornet PAVE LOWs aboard the USS *Peleliu* for deployment to the Operation Enduring Freedom theatre. In the foreground is s/n 69-5794. (Sean Borland)

## Chapter 6: Sandstorms

A SEAL Desert Patrol Vehicle (DPV) is loaded aboard a 20th SOS MH-53 for use in Iraq. DPVs are fast, agile, and heavily armed dune buggies used for long range recon and downed aircrew rescue. (Sean Borland)

flies the MH-53J/M, relinquished the support mission due to its move from RAF Alconbury to RAF Mildenhall, United Kingdom. The third squadron in the Air Force Special Operations Command flying the MH-53J/M is the 31st SOS based at Osan AB, South Korea. While flying in support of Operations Provide Promise and Deny Flight in Bosnia-Herzegovina in 1995, 20th SOS Pave Low crews flew a high-risk attempt to rescue two French fliers. The following year, Green Hornet crews were involved in the search for the crash of an aircraft carrying Commerce Secretary Ronald Brown and his entourage. Those same crews shortly thereafter flew in support of American Embassy evacuations in Monrovia, Liberia, airlifting more than 2,000 evacuees.

Although Pave Lows are expected to be replaced by Bell/Boeing CV-22 Ospreys by 2007, the MH-53s' retirement is well distant. New systems comprising an interactive defensive avionics system and multi-mission advanced tactical terminal (IDAS/MATT) resulted in the designation MH-53M. The system not only enhances defensive and detection avoidance capabilities, it presents a real-time picture of the battlefield. The first MH-53M Pave Low IV was delivered to the 20th SOS on 17 April 1998. Beginning in 2000, the fleet of MH-53s underwent modification with a Lockheed Martin-designed digital/glass cockpit. In July 2001 the last four TH-53As, which had been acquired from the Marines in 1988 for training Pave Low crews, were retired. They were replaced in the 58th SOW at Kirtland AFB by Pave Lows transferred from the 31st SOS. As of this writing, a total of 13 MH-53Js and 25 MH-53Ms exist in the Air Force inventory. As the largest and most technologically advanced helicopter in the Air Force, the MH-53J/

Navy F-14 pilot Lt. Devon Jones dashes for the safety of a 20th SOS MH-53, which made the rescue after Jones and Lawrence Slade were shot down deep inside Iraq in January 1991. Slade had been captured. This was the first combat rescue behind enemy lines since the Vietnam war. (U.S. Air Force)

## Green Hornets: The History of the U.S. Air Force 20th Special Operations Squadron

Manning a minigun, this MH-53 "tail gunner" wears a modern version of the "monkey harness" to keep him tethered to the aircraft during violent maneuvers. (Sean Borland)

M boasts a maximum takeoff weight of 46,000 pounds, and it has a cruise speed of 165 mph. Power is supplied by a pair of General Electric T-64GE/-100 engines.

Learning to fly the Pave Low is an eight-month experience in confidence building. Eighty percent of training sorties are flown at night. Missions are routinely flown at the dangerous height of 50 feet above the ground, and in bad weather. Former Green Hornet pilot Lt. Col. Gene Correll states:

"You take off those night vision goggles and fly strictly on instruments to develop confidence. And you continually practice it. We don't chase the moon cycle, like in the early days of night vision goggles. Now with the Pave Low system and the radar, we go out any night. It's the greatest challenge anyone will face in any aircraft."

Typical of those who challenged themselves is Captain Sean M. Borland, who became an MH-53M Weapons Instructor Pilot in 2004:

"I inter-service transferred to the USAF along with several other pilots from the U.S. Army in July 1999. I attended Officer

A 20th SOS MH-53 performs a "Helocast," which is the deployment of special operations swimmers and boats. The maneuver is called "low and slow," because it is done no higher than ten feet above the water, and at ten knots ground speed. Often the rear ramp is actually placed in the water. (Sean Borland)

## Chapter 6: Sandstorms

A trio of 20th SOS MH-53s departs Eglin's Field 6 during a training mission during the late 1990s. (U.S. Air Force)

The ultimate special operations aircraft, the MH-53M. (Author's Collection)

## Green Hornets: The History of the U.S. Air Force 20th Special Operations Squadron

Training School, various survival schools, and the MH-53J Mission Qualification Course. I was previously a rated Army attack helicopter pilot and flew the AH-1F, and I was an AH-64A Instructor Pilot. My first USAF assignment was to the 20th Special Operations Squadron 'Green Hornets' in October 2000 as an MH-53J/M pilot. I was very excited to be assigned to the 20th. The squadron was considered 'The Show,' and has a long and distinguished history. It's a large squadron, and in the year before 9/11 it seemed like its three different flights were always on the road for training.

My first six months in the 20th included working off the *USS Eisenhower* for the Joint Shipboard Helicopter Integration Process (JSIP), flying in *Red Flag 01-03*, and a manning assist temporary duty to the 31st SOS for exercise *Tandem Thrust 2001* in Australia. I completed my first pilot upgrade (FP) in July, and enjoyed learning the 20th's tactical mission, and working with the various special operations ground 'customers.'

The world changed drastically for the 20th SOS, as it did for all Americans, on 9/11/01. The 20th immediately deployed crews and aircraft to assist initial recovery operations in New York and Washington, D.C. I was in the alert flight, called A Flight, 20th SOS. We deployed aboard the *USS Peleliu* to a classified location in the Middle East, and then executed Combat Search and Rescue (CSAR) alert for the first strikes of *Operation Enduring Freedom*. This was the beginning of the numerous missions the 20th flew in support of *Enduring Freedom*. The missions included multiple infiltration, exfiltration, and re-supply missions in support of special operations ground forces operating in Afghanistan. The deployment schedule was relentless, but no one complained, because we

The time-honored minigun continues to provide muscle for Green Hornet helicopters. Pictured here is the MH-53's right side GAU-2A/B in the stowed position. (Dale Robinson)

Firepower for modern Green Hornet helicopters also takes the form of the .50 cal. machine gun, which is often used interchangeably with the minigun. The fearsome .50 cal. weapon made a comeback in armed aircraft during the 21st century. (Author's Collection)

## Chapter 6: Sandstorms

This 20th SOS MH-53J, s/n 68-10924, was converted from a CH-53C. (U.S. Air Force)

all realized what we were there for. In the fall of 2002 our focus turned towards a new threat: Iraq.

The entire 20th SOS deployed in early 2003 to prepare for combat operations in what is now known as *Operation Iraqi Freedom (OIF)*. The Green Hornets have flown, and continue to fly a variety of missions in OIF, including the seizure of the Al Faw Peninsula Oil Fields. The mission prevented an ecological disaster like the one that occurred during *Operation Desert Storm*. It was an outstanding mission, and I had the opportunity to be the *Chalk Two* aircraft commander. I attribute the success of the mission to the detailed tactical planning and rehearsals conducted by the flight lead, and professional execution by the eight crews who flew the mission.

I had the opportunity to fly as an aircraft commander for the Hurricane Katrina evacuation of New Orleans. This was the most rewarding mission of my military career. The first mission on 2 September 2005 supported President Bush's visit to New Orleans. I flew back-up to *Marine One* over downtown New Orleans. My second mission was on 4 September. We flew from sunrise until well after dark, using the MH-53's heavy lift capabilities to evacuate people from the various collection point landing zones to the New Orleans International Airport. The largest group of evacuees was at the New Orleans convention center parking lot. It was a challenging landing zone surrounded by power lines and a 200-foot overpass. My crew evacuated 176 people, 4 dogs, 2 cats, and 2 birds that day. Every Green Hornet crew was focused on getting the evacuees safely and rapidly to the airport. The totals for 20th SOS support to Hurricane Katrina was 1,395 people evacuated, 10 dogs, 2 cats, 2 birds, 7,750 pounds of cargo transported, and 134 hours flown.

I'm very proud to have been a member of the 20th SOS. I hope to be a Green Hornet again flying the CV-22. Our motto: 'Once a Hornet, always a Hornet!'"

# Green Hornets: The History of the U.S. Air Force 20th Special Operations Squadron

20th SOS MH-53s fly over flood ravaged New Orleans in the aftermath of Hurricane Katrina. Green Hornet helicopters played a major role in evacuating those stranded by the flood. (Sean Borland)

Green Hornet flight engineer SSGT. P.J. Fraley has this to say:

"When you're flying low, yankin' and bankin' in the trees and the dirt, it's a great feeling. It's exciting. You're one step away from the threshold all the time. Down low. That's where the action is!"

And that's where the 20th SOS Green Hornets likely will always be.

# Warriors

20th Helicopter Squadron gunners Harding (left) and Ludnigson in 1967. (Tom Garcia)

Michael W. Bedwell, armed with a CAR-15, M-60A, and .38 cal. Revolver, in 1967. (Michael Bedwell Collection)

*Green Hornets: The History of the U.S. Air Force 20th Special Operations Squadron*

A SOG Recon Team leader and one of his indigenous charges prior to boarding a Green Hornet Huey in 1967. Both carry AK-47 rifles. (Tom Garcia)

20th crewmen Tom Booth (left) and Jim Bedingfield at Duc Lap. (James Bedingfield Collection)

# Warriors

Captain Swank. (Rich Jalloway)

Captain Woidke. (Rich Jalloway)

*Green Hornets: The History of the U.S. Air Force 20th Special Operations Squadron*

Captain Robert Burton. (Rich Jalloway)

Unidentified Green Hornet pilot. (Rich Jalloway)

## Warriors

December 1971. (James R. Wagner)

Future warriors? Montagnard children pose with Green Hornet weaponry at Ban Me Thuot in 1970. (James Pedriana)

*Green Hornets: The History of the U.S. Air Force 20th Special Operations Squadron*

Special Forces sergeant and the camp mascot "Susie" atop a bunker at Duc Lap in 1968. (James Tolbert)

# Warriors

Green Hornet pilot Edward K. McGuire. (James R. Wagner)

Pony Express pilot Major Kyron V. Hall (Kyron V. Hall Collection)

## Green Hornets: The History of the U.S. Air Force 20th Special Operations Squadron

Unidentified senior officer. (Rich Jalloway)

Sergeants Rich Jalloway and Jim Fudge at Thieu Atar in 1971. Barely visible on the UH-1N's nose is a slogan of the times: "Keep on Truckin'." (Rich Jalloway Collection)

## Warriors

After legendary SOG Sergeant Jerry Shriver went missing in action, Green Hornet crews looked after his dog, "Klaus," seen here at Ban Me Thuot in September 1971. At far right is Tom Fike, who was killed in action three months later. (James R. Wagner)

Michael Mullen. (David Galvan)

Colonel Stephen Von Phul. (Author's Collection)

Sergeant Robert D. Hill in 1968. (Robert Hill Collection)

# Warriors

Green Hornet gunner SGT Gardinier. (James R. Wagner)

Indigenous SOG soldiers pose with a 20th SOS mechanic in a UH-1P at Ban Me Thuot in 1971. (Rich Jalloway)

# Green Hornets: The History of the U.S. Air Force 20th Special Operations Squadron

Rich Jalloway at Duc Lap in 1971. (Rich Jalloway Collection)

Captain James R. Tolbert with a UH-1P in 1968. (James Tolbert Collection)

# Warriors

SSGT Jim Burns poses with the 21st CH-3C named "Mother Bare" at NKP in 1969. (James Burns Collection)

Captain Len Cormney, gunship Instructor Pilot and Flight Examiner. (James R. Wagner)

*Green Hornets: The History of the U.S. Air Force 20th Special Operations Squadron*

Thomas Fike, the last Green Hornet to be killed in action during the Vietnam war. (Rich Jalloway)

# Warriors

SGT Tom Kreidler. (Tom Kreidler Collection)

Captain Phillip Miller. (James R. Wagner)

UH-1N crew in 1971. (Rich Jalloway)

## Warriors

James A. Losness. (Rich Jalloway)

Airman Bryan R. McGregor. (Rich Jalloway)

Billy Tedford. (Rich Jalloway)

A1C William B. Higgins. (Rich Jalloway)

## Warriors

Durion D. Penn, Life Support Shop in 1971. (Rich Jalloway)

SGT Clyde R. Ficklin and friends. (Rich Jalloway)

*Green Hornets: The History of the U.S. Air Force 20th Special Operations Squadron*

Dennis C. Bowling. (Rich Jalloway)

John J. Snider. (Rich Jalloway)

# Warriors

Jerry L. Lechien. (Rich Jalloway)

Left to right: Jack G. Woodson, Donald Douglas, and Kelly McGuire. (Rich Jalloway)

*Green Hornets: The History of the U.S. Air Force 20th Special Operations Squadron*

Harold Alkire, Jr. (Rich Jalloway)

Frank Waid. (Rich Jalloway)

# Warriors

Jesus Jeminez in 1971. (Rich Jalloway)

Morris T. Beaver (left) and Richard Van Der Ploeg. (Rich Jalloway)

# Green Hornets: The History of the U.S. Air Force 20th Special Operations Squadron

Joseph H. Sanchez (left) and Joseph Roman. (Rich Jalloway)

Alex H. Gay III. (Rich Jalloway)

# Warriors

Jimmy D. Brady. (Rich Jalloway)

Darrell L. Babb. (Rich Jalloway)

Eugene C. Kopf. (Rich Jalloway)

Lt. Col. Robert Madison at Cam Ranh Bay in 1971. (James R. Wagner)

## Warriors

SGT Jon D. Harston, who later became a CH-53 crewman and earned the Air Force Cross for the Mayaguez mission on 15 May 1975. (Rich Jalloway)

Gunner Gerald Ciochon in 1971. (Rich Jalloway)

*Green Hornets: The History of the U.S. Air Force 20th Special Operations Squadron*

Edward Hollingsworth. (Rich Jalloway)

Joseph V. Wildinger. (Rich Jalloway)

# Warriors

Captain James H. Partridge in June 1971. (Rich Jalloway)

Paul R. Jensen. (Rich Jalloway)

*Green Hornets: The History of the U.S. Air Force 20th Special Operations Squadron*

Aimo Jarvi. (Rich Jalloway)

SSGT Alfonse R. "RT" Torres at Duc Lap in October 1970. (James Green)

# Warriors

Montagnard ("Yard") SOG Recon Team soldier, armed with an M-14, at Duc Co in 1968. (James Tolbert)

# Green Hornets: The History of the U.S. Air Force 20th Special Operations Squadron

Dante E. Biagi, Jr. (left) and Richard P. Lessentine pose with "Echo." (Rich Jalloway)

UH-1P crew chief James Pedriana at Ban Me Thuot in July 1970. (James Pedriana Collection)

*Warriors*

James R. Wagner in 1971. (James R. Wagner Collection)

# Green Hornets: The History of the U.S. Air Force 20th Special Operations Squadron

Gunner SGT Wilkerson and trusted companion in 1970. (James Green)

Captain Bud Jenkins straps into a UH-1N at Cam Ranh Bay in 1971. (James Green)

*Green Hornets: The History of the U.S. Air Force 20th Special Operations Squadron*

SSGT David Galvan at Tuy Hoa in 1970. (James Green)

Green Hornet pilots Captains William Rowell (left) and Sean Borland in Afghanistan. Markings immediately behind the pilot's window indicate a bullet hole. Borland notes: "It was a pretty interesting evening." (Sean Borland Collection)

*Warriors*

MH-53 tail gunner Kensey in Afghanistan. (Sean Borland)

# Green Hornets: The History of the U.S. Air Force 20th Special Operations Squadron

This "Moccasin" 20th SOS crew, seen here in June 1991, rescued a Navy F-14 pilot during Operation Desert Storm. (Sean Borland)

"Crew Two" in Afghanistan. (Sean Borland)

## Warriors

The 20th SOS in Afghanistan in summer 2002. (Sean Borland Collection)

The Green Hornets hold a reunion at Kokomo, Indiana, every September. (Rich Jalloway)

# Emblems

*Emblems*

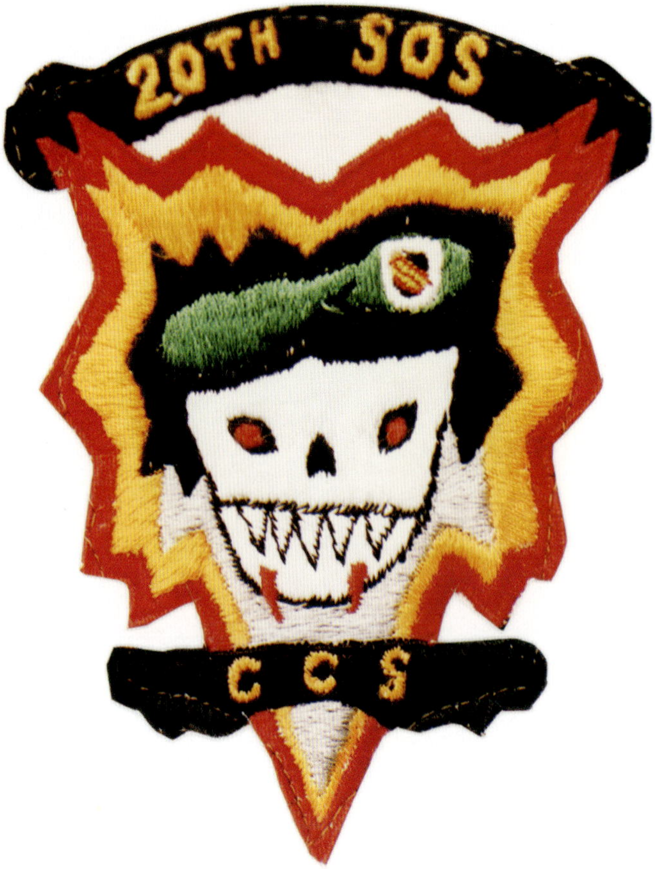
20TH SOS
CCS

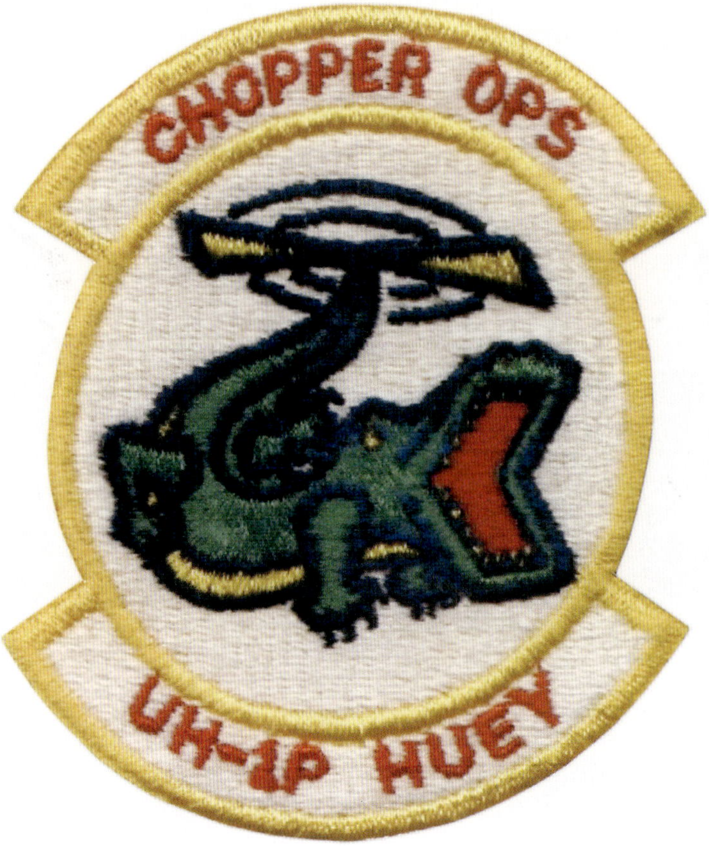
CHOPPER OPS
UH-1P HUEY

*Emblems*

56th SPECIAL OPERATIONS WING

GREEN HORNETS
20TH SPECIAL OPERATIONS SQ

*Emblems*

*Green Hornets: The History of the U.S. Air Force 20th Special Operations Squadron*

*Emblems*

*Green Hornets: The History of the U.S. Air Force 20th Special Operations Squadron*

*Emblems*

20TH SOS
GREEN HORNETS

SPECIAL OPERATIONS FORCES
MH-53J
Pave Low III E
ANY TIME
ANY PLACE
LORAL AN/ALQ-157 IRCM
The Ultimate Distraction

Emblems

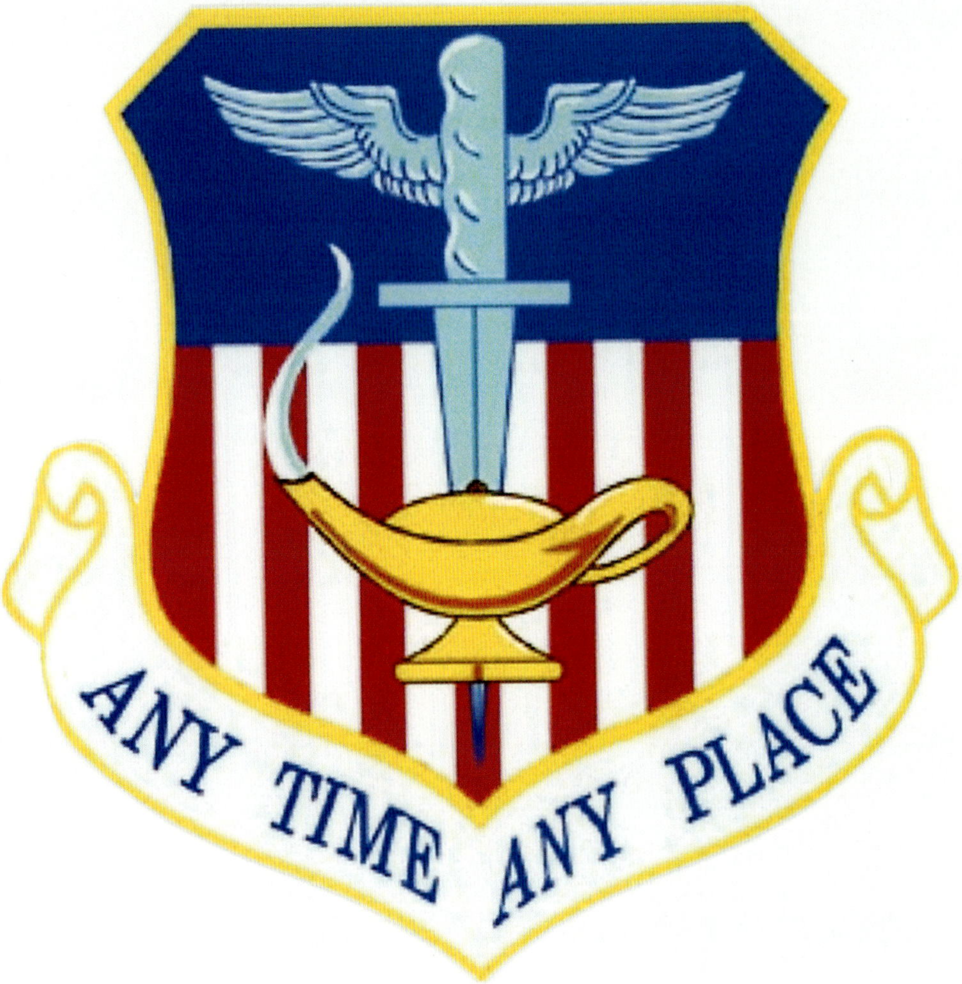
ANY TIME ANY PLACE

# Appendix A:
# Sikorsky CH-3C/E Helicopters Assigned to the 20th HS/SOS

| Serial Number | Notes |
| --- | --- |
| 62-12579 | destroyed by ground fire in Laos on 10 June 1969 |
| 62-12582 | lost at LS-36 TACAN site in Laos on 17 January 1969 |
| 63-9676 | "Black Mariah;" to USAF Museum |
| 63-9678 | destroyed in Laos on 30 December 1967 |
| 63-9681 | shot down with 21st SOS in Thailand on 13 August 1970; four crew KIA |
| 63-9682 | destroyed in Laos on 20 February 1969 |
| 63-9689 | crashed during night mission on 19 January 1969 |
| 63-9690 | |
| 63-9691 | |
| 64-14221 | |
| 64-14222 | |
| 64-14236 | destroyed Laos 23 August 1967 |
| 64-14237 | destroyed 26 February 1969 |
| 65-15691 | shot down in Laos on 27 June 1969 |
| 65-15692 | |
| 65-15693 | |
| 65-15695 | |
| 65-15697 | |
| 66-13287 | lost with 21st SOS on 24 October 1970; two crew KIA |
| 66-13291 | |
| 66-13295 | lost in South Vietnam with 21st SOS on 23 May 1968; five crew KIA |
| 69-5811 | J-CATCH |

# Appendix B:
# Bell UH-1F/P Helicopters Assigned to the 20th HS/SOS

| Serial Number | Notes |
|---|---|
| 63-13146 | storage 12 December 1973 |
| 63-13149 | storage 23 December 1987 |
| 63-13150 | storage 1989 |
| 63-13151 | lost on 19 May 1969 |
| 63-13152 | shot down in Cambodia on 21 April 1969 attempting SF team extraction |
| 63-13154 |  |
| 63-13155 | lost on 21 October 1969 |
| 63-13158 | shot down in South Vietnam on 26 March 1969; seven aboard KIA |
| 63-13159 | written off |
| 63-13160 | to 35th TFW; storage 7 April 1980 |
| 63-13161 | storage 1989 |
| 63-13162 | storage 25 November 1977 |
| 63-13163 | to 57th FWW; storage |
| 63-13164 | shot down in Cambodia on 3 January 1969; one crewman KIA |
| 63-13165 |  |
| 64-15476 | USAF Museum display |
| 64-15484 | arrived from 317th SOS at Hurlburt Field on 17 June 1970; crashed and burned avoiding mid-air with VNAF H-34 on 25 September 1970; two crewmen KIA and two wounded |
| 64-15486 | arrived Vietnam 30 June 1970; storage |
| 64-15491 | shot down at Duc Lap 14 March 1970, pilot KIA |
| 64-15492 | lost 13 February 1969, Fleming's MOH aircraft |
| 64-15493 | display at Hurlburt early 1981 |

## Appendix B: Bell UH-1F/P Helicopters Assigned to the 20th HS/SOS

| | |
|---|---|
| 65-7916 | storage |
| 65-7925 | display at Museum of Aviation, Warner Robins AFB |
| 65-7926 | arrived Vietnam from Howard AFB 30 June 1970; storage |
| 65-7927 | written off |
| 65-7928 | arrived Vietnam from Hurlburt 17 June 1970; storage |
| 65-7929 | storage 1977 |
| 65-7930 | shot down during gunnery training in South Vietnam on 29 July 1970; five aboard injured; aircraft recovered but written off |
| 65-7931 | written off |
| 65-7932 | crashed following ground fire during SF re-supply near Dak To, South Vietnam on 31 March 1967; pilot KIA |
| 65-7935 | lost on 8 December 1969 |
| 65-7936 | storage |
| 65-7937 | shot down during extraction near Pleiku, South Vietnam on 13 April 1969; pilot KIA; two crewmen wounded |
| 65-7939 | written off |
| 65-7942 | shot down during extraction near Duc Co, South Vietnam on 27 November 1968; one crewman KIA |
| 65-7943 | |
| 65-7944 | shot down during two-ship training flight at Dar Lac near Ban Me Thuot on 19 March 1970; three crewmen KIA |
| 65-7948 | arrived Vietnam from Howard AFB on 30 June 1970; storage |

# Appendix C:
# Bell UH-1N Helicopters Assigned to the 20th SOS

| Serial Number | Notes |
|---|---|
| 69-6604 | |
| 69-6611 | |
| 69-6612 | |
| 69-6613 | |
| 69-6614 | |
| 69-6615 | |
| 69-6616 | |
| 69-6617 | |
| 69-6618 | |
| 69-6619 | |
| 69-6620 | |
| 69-6621 | shot down on 4 December 1971 in South Vietnam; one crewman KIA; aircraft recovered, but shot down in Cambodia on 3 February 1972; destroyed by A-1 Skyraiders |
| 69-6622 | |
| 69-6624 | |
| 69-6625 | |
| 69-6626 | |
| 69-6627 | |
| 69-6628 | |
| 69-6629 | |
| 69-6631 | lost due to tail rotor failure off coast of South Vietnam on 18 October 1971; both pilots injured |
| 69-6632 | |

# Appendix C: Bell UH-1N Helicopters Assigned to the 20th SOS

69-6633

69-6641

69-6642       1st SOW 1970s

69-6644       lost at sea off Bahamas 1984 due to mechanical failure; five aboard killed and four injured

69-6653

69-6654

# Appendix D:
# Sikorsky H-53 Helicopters Assigned to the 20th SOS

| Serial Number | Notes |
| --- | --- |
| 66-14428 | later 551st SOS |
| 66-14429 | later 551st SOS |
| 66-14431 | operational loss in 1988 while assigned to 551st SOS |
| 66-14432 | later 551st SOS |
| 66-14433 | prototype HH-53H; later to 551st SOS |
| 67-14993 | combat loss Iraq on 19 March 2003; destroyed to prevent capture |
| 67-14994 | first MH-53J rollout on 17 July 1987 |
| 67-14995 | ex HH-53C; flight lead during "Vega 31" and "Hammer 34" rescue missions in Serbia during *Operation Allied Force* |
| 68-8284 | ex HH-53C |
| 68-8286 | ex HH-53C; Son Tay raid as "Apple Three;" battle damaged in Southeast Asia; crashed near Ft. Pickett, Virginia in 1988; combat loss in Afghanistan in March 2002; named "Nine Lives" |
| 68-10356 | ex HH-53C; *Desert Storm* first mission; first coalition aircraft at Kuwait City IAP; first coalition aircraft at U.S. embassy in Kuwait City |
| 68-10357 | lead aircraft on Son Tay raid as "Apple One;" named "Magnum" with 20th SOS |
| 68-10358 | ex HH-53C |
| 68-10360 | ex HH-53C |
| 68-10364 | ex HH-53C; assault on Koh Tang Island as "Jolly Green Eleven; first MH-53J in combat and received ground fire over Panama City during *Operation Just Cause* on 20 December 1989; crashed and was destroyed at Hurlburt Field on 2 June 1999 - one Army Ranger killed |
| 68-10367 | ex HH-53C; *Operation Just Cause*, Panama; led first mission of *Desert Storm* in January 1991 |
| 68-10369 | ex HH-53C; first mission of *Desert Storm*; named "The Love Machine" with 20th SOS |
| 68-10923 | one of two CH-53Cs converted to HH/MH-53H; later to 551st SOS |
| 68-10924 | ex CH-53C |

# Appendix D: Sikorsky H-53 Helicopters Assigned to the 20th SOS

| | |
|---|---|
| 68-10928 | assault on Koh Tang Island in may 1975 as "Knife 22" |
| 68-10930 | first successful combat rescue since Vietnam "Slate 46" pickup during *Desert Storm*; operational loss in Iraq in February 2003 |
| 69-5785 | ex HH-53C; assault on Koh Tang Island as "Jolly Green Two" May 1975 |
| 69-5789 | ex HH-53C |
| 69-5790 | ex HH/MH-53H |
| 69-5791 | first production HH-53H; operational loss in Afghanistan in November 2001 |
| 69-5793 | assault on Koh Tang Island as "Jolly Green Twelve" |
| 69-5794 | ex HH-53C. Assault on Koh Tang Island as "Jolly Green Thirteen" |
| 69-5795 | ex HH-53C; assault on Koh Tang Island as "Jolly Green Forty One;" crashed in Arabian Desert during *Operation Desert Shield*; later to 20th SOS |
| 69-5797 | ex HH-53c; shot down in Iraq with rocket propelled grenade (RPG) during March 2004 - destroyed to prevent capture |
| 70-1625 | ex CH-53C; "Chalk Two" during "Hammer 34" rescue mission in Serbia during *Operation Allied Force*; made first night landing at Buckingham Palace in November 2003 in support of President Bush's visit to England; operational loss on 23 November 2003 after takeoff from FOB - four aircrew and one SOF member killed |
| 70-1629 | one of two CH-53cs converted to HH/MH-53 |
| 70-1630 | ex CH-53C; flew first *Desert Storm* mission |
| 70-1631 | ex CH-53C |
| 73-1647 | ex HH-53C and HH/MH-53H; operational loss on 17 October 1984 near Clark AB, Philippines - crashed in heavy rain squall at night during *Exercise Cope Thunder* - all aboard killed |
| 73-1648 | ex HH/MH-53H; crashed during exercise in September 1987, killing an Army Ranger; later to 20th SOS |
| 73-1650 | ex HH-53C and HH/MH-53H; mechanical loss in November 1984 near Pope AFB, North Carolina, when tail rotor separated in flight |
| 73-1651 | ex HH-53C and HH/MH-53H; flew Jonestown, Guyana mission in November 1978; operational loss on 21 May 1986 near Nellis AFB, Nevada - crashed during night formation approach during *Exercise Elated Cyclone* |
| 73-1652 | ex HH-53C and HH./MH-53H; flew Jonestown, Guyana mission in November 1978 |

NOTE: All original U.S. Air Force HH-53Bs, HH-53Cs, and CH-53Cs were converted to HH/MH-53Hs. This list does not include CH/NCH/TH-53As obtained from the U.S. Marine Corps.

# Bibliography

Mutza, Wayne. *UH-1 Huey In Action*. Squadron Signal Publications: Carrollton, TX, 1986.

Van Staaveren, Jacob. *Interdiction in Southern Laos 1960-1968*. Center for Air Force History: Washington, D.C., 1993.

**Government Publications**

*Flight Manual U.S.A.F. Series UH-1N Helicopter T.O. 1H-1 (U)N-1*, September 1973.

U.S.A.F. AF Form 642 *Medal of Honor Recommendation for 1st LT. James P. Fleming*. David K. Sparks, Lt. Col., USAF.

U.S.A.F. *Historical Report, 20th SOS 1 October-31 December 1968*.

U.S.A.F. *Historical Reports, 20th SOS - Quarterlies 1971*.

U.S.A.F. *Historical Reports, 20th SOS - April through December 1971*.

U.S.A.F. *History 14th Special Operations Wing, Nha Trang AB, RVN 1 October-31 December 1968*. Project Corona Harvest.

U.S.A.F. *Project CHECO Southeast Asia Report; The Royal Thai Air Force,* (date classified).

**Magazines**

Air Enthusiast No. 32. Mutza, Wayne, *Covertly to Cambodia*. 1987.

AIRMAN
    Blair, Ed, *A Fight for Life*. February, 1970.
    Rhodes, Phil, TSGT, *Special Operations: Swift and Silent*. October 1991.
    Sturm, Ted R., *Miracle at the River*. June 1970.
    *The Pony Rides in Vegas*. April 1981.

Newsweek. Waller, Douglas, *Secret Warriors*. June 17, 1991.

TAC ATTACK. Vallimont, Joe, *J-Catch*. March 1979.

The Commando. Marotte, Dawn, A1C, *White House Recognizes the 20th Special Operations Squadron*. March 1, 1985.

Vietnam. Robinson, Dale K., TSGT, USAF (Ret.), *20th Special Operations Squadron Air Commandos*. August 1998.

## Loach!
### The Story of the H-6/Model 500 Helicopter
**Wayne Mutza**

Don't be fooled by the small size of the H-6/Model 500 helicopter. In the scout role in Vietnam, OH-6As and their aircrew became legends for their high-risk work in the low-level environment. Wayne Mutza presents the small, dynamic helicopter's story in this well-written, superbly detailed, and lavishly illustrated volume. Much of the OH-6A's combat record in Vietnam is told in firsthand accounts. Mutza offers fascinating insight to the helicopter's controversial beginning, its development, and its service with the Army National Guard, the Army's flight demonstration team, worldwide operators, and law enforcement agencies. In addition, the reader is treated to an entire chapter devoted to the Little Birds of Special Operations. Also included are appendices with factual data, and more than sixty emblems. It's all here in this highly readable volume.

| | | |
|---|---|---|
| Size: 8 1/2" x 11" | over 300 color and b/w photographs | 144 pages |
| ISBN: 0764323431 | Soft Cover | $29.95 |

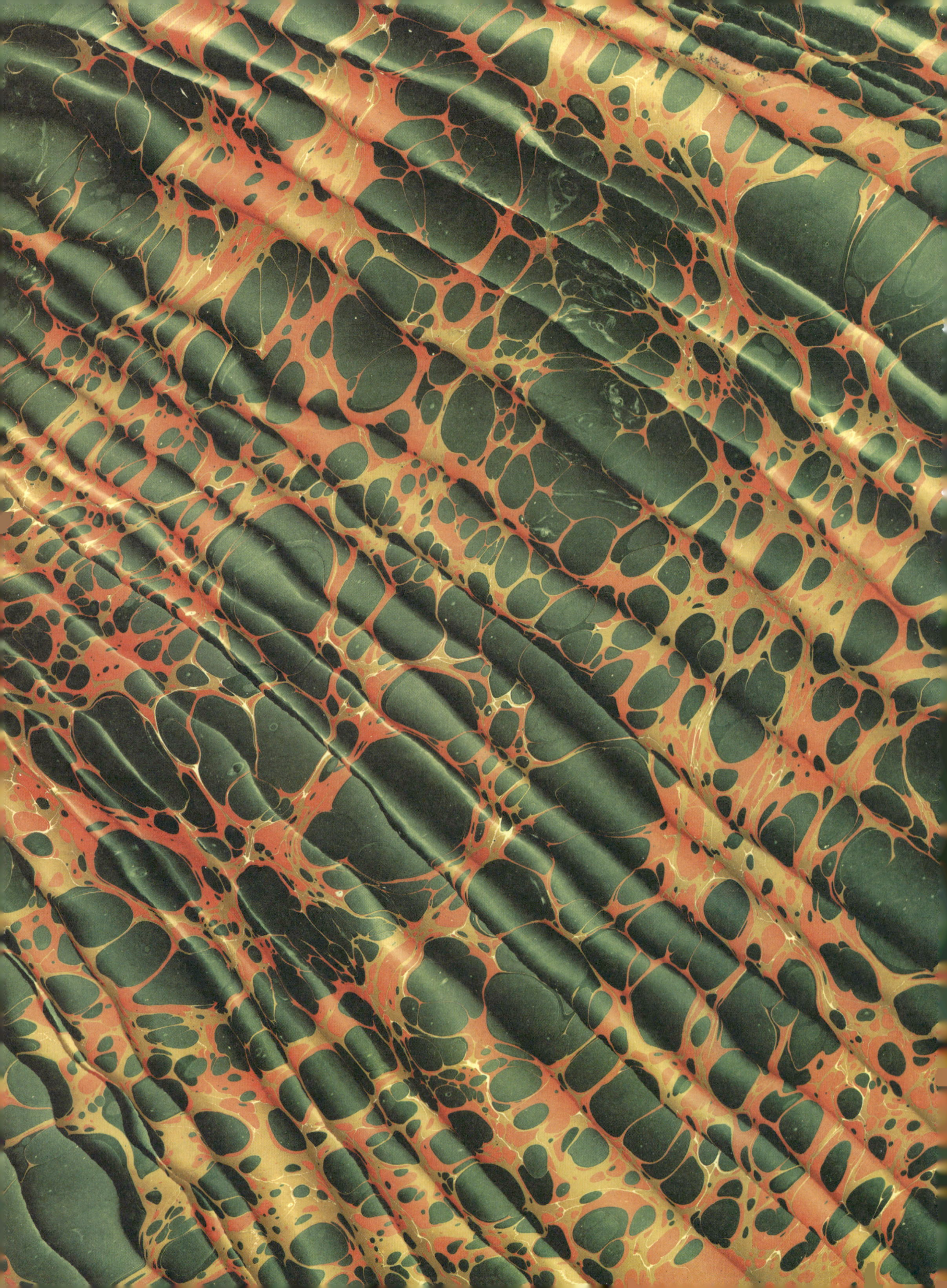